KT-417-706

A

CHAT ROUND

THE

OLD COURSE

A
CHAT ROUND
THE
OLD COURSE

BY

D.D.R.O.

SPORTSPRINT PUBLISHING

EDINBURGH

With apologies to the Saturday foursome and others

© D.D.R.O. 1990

All rights reserved.

No part of this publication may be reproduced
in any form or by any means without
the prior permission of the publishers,
John Donald Publishers Ltd.,
138 St Stephen Street, Edinburgh EH3 5AA

ISBN 0 85976 311 0

British Library Cataloguing in Publication Data
D. D. R. O.
A chat round the old course.
1. Scotland. Fife Region. St Andrews: Old
course, history
I. Title
796.35206841292

Phototypeset by Beecee Typesetting Services
Printed and bound in Great Britain by Bell & Bain Ltd., Glasgow

CONTENTS

FOREWORD

HAVING PLAYED, AND CHATTED, ROUND THE Old Course at St Andrews for thirty years and more, I've come to know it rather well — even its less accessible parts. Quite often I've been approached on the first tee by a stranger who, with the connivance of the Starter, asks if he might join me. So far, it has always been a 'he', since ladies seldom turn up unannounced and never, it seems, unchaperoned. He has probably come half way round the world for the privilege (of playing the Old, not necessarily with me) and is normally a trifle nervous as well as, for a couple of holes at least, deferential.

Once it was an Australian, of mature years, who put a large chunk of his life's savings into his pilgrimage to the Home of Golf. Having hired a set of clubs and squared the Starter (with what subtle persuasion I know not), he joined me on the first tee, begging me to open the proceedings. The very act of stepping onto the sacred turf was for him an almost mystical experience. Perhaps it was the feeling of being glared at by the great window of the Royal and Ancient Club, wide as the eye of the deity, that made him especially agitated. Anyway, once I had modestly despatched my ball down the fairway, he fumbled for a tee and, with great reverence, pressed it almost apologetically into the turf. Shyly he removed the driver from his bag and then — oh, horror! — found he had forgotten to obtain any balls. It was no hardship for me to come to his rescue, as well-worn balls seem to breed in my bag. So I found one with *ST ANDREWS* stamped across it, gave it a much-needed scrub in the ball-washer, and handed it to him with my compliments and some sympathy. He had at least remembered to take a card of the course from the Starter; and as we played our round, he conscientiously entered his score for every hole. When we left the eighteenth green, he did his addition, and was delighted to find that it came to a round hundred. So he dated the card and had me sign it. Later, after some convivial formalities, he took my address. Some time afterwards I received a letter from him, saying what a thrill for him the occasion had been, and adding that he had had the card framed and the ball mounted, both now being on display in his home club.

When I curse the obvious strangers in the match ahead for their leisurely pace and, as often as not, cinematography, I often remember my Australian friend and his transcendental experience (not that he lingered unduly over it). And that makes me a little more forgiving than I might otherwise be.

It was after watching such adventurers peering this way and that and consulting the map of the course on their cards that the idea for this book came to me. People who write accounts of how to play the Old Course always seem to direct them at players whose handicaps are no larger than the number on the ball they are playing with. Surely, I thought, they could address themselves to someone more like me (my own handicap has covered the range between 18 and 7 and is now well on its way up again). So I had the notion of conjuring up another antipodean partner prepared, like the first, to bear with my reminiscences, provided I leavened them with a few tips by way of introduction to the caprices of this mother of all golf courses. Should you care to eavesdrop as we play round it hole by hole, I hope you too may derive some benefit and pleasure, if not from the conversation, then at least from catching a whiff of the bracing links air. But enough of that: let's pay our dues and get to the teeing ground.

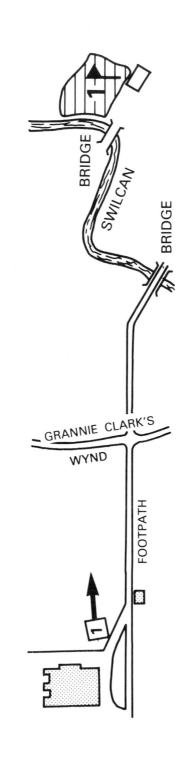

HOLE 1

THE BURN

O N THE FIRST TEE YOU MUST BE ON YOUR BEST behaviour, which basically means you don't take practice swings and don't drive until you hear the Starter's voice, suitably amplified for the occasion, inviting (no, bidding) you to 'Play away, please!' And best not use an iron — I've known one incumbent of the Starter's Box object strongly to that. Oh, and don't look round: you might be discomfited by a seemingly critical gaze from THAT window. And how could you know that it belongs not to someone at Jehovah's right hand, but to an all too human Member of the Royal and Ancient drowning his sorrows after an abysmal round on the New?

So off you go, keeping well left, especially if you're inclined to slice; though you might wait until that cyclist is off the road (why on earth is he pushing his bike instead of riding it?). Don't worry about the foursome playing the eighteenth: I'll shout 'fore' if necessary. That's it· aim over there. The worst that can happen is a hook that will put you under the windows of the New Club; or of the St Andrews Club, if it's really short. — Well not quite the worst: a friend of mine playing his first round on the Old got one off the heel and disturbed some folk putting out on the last green. Which is even more difficult to achieve than a complete air shot. But you'd really better drive now: the Starter doesn't like repeating himself. — Oh, good hit! — Fore! — It's all right. I don't think it hurt her: she seems well padded just there.

She did take a bit of the run off, though. In any case, as you say you're not a long hitter, it's best not to go for the green with your second. Just take a short iron and leave it a few yards from the Swilcan Burn and well left of the pin: then you should have a short shot to the hole with plenty of green to work with. And if you happen to thin it, it won't finish in the heavy rough behind the green. That's a bad place to be, because if you again catch it thin or there's a strong wind from the west, you can easily run back across the green and into the burn. — That's the way. Now you've a longish putt for your par, or anyway an easy five, unless you putt like me.

*   *   *

I KNOW WHAT A NERVE-RACKING EXPERIENCE it can be to take your first drive on the Old Course. In my case I think it was the second occasion that turned into a veritable nightmare. It was a beautiful summer afternoon, and I'd been honoured by two eminent professors asking me to join them for a game. We arrived on the tee under the eyes of crowds of idling holidaymakers and were called to play away by the notoriously fierce Starter of the time. My humble station demanded that I should drive third, following two very presentable shots by my seniors. I teed up, addressed the ball and prepared to initiate a swing more elegantly controlled than my customary heave. But then, out of the corner of my left eye, I saw a woman walking slowly from Grannie Clark's Wynd into my area of operations. She was, moreover, pushing a pram! Not being by nature an infanticide, I held my fire and pulled myself up from the crouch I call my stance. The domestic group proceeded gently on its way. Then, on the direct line between tee and green, it came to a halt. My companions shouted 'Fore!': I was speechless. The Starter felt the call of duty and with his well-known stentorian voice adopted the role of choir leader. The woman was by now bending over the pram, quite oblivious to the part she was playing in this developing drama. Casual bystanders, no doubt welcoming the chance of participating in events on this illustrious golfing stage, added more vocal lines to the swelling chorus. The woman was   now

12

LECKIE

rummaging in the depths of the pram. The Starter followed his bellow out of his box and began to stride towards her. At that moment she straightened up and waved a white rectangle to no one in particular. Flag of surrender? No a soggy nappy! And with her maternal duty done, she proceeded with measured tread towards the beach I resumed my address, knees knocking, teeth chattering, and a mist before my eyes. Then, believe it or not, I actually hit the ball in more or less the right direction.

Another long wait I once had on that tee was occasioned by two American lady 'golfers' (the term is used loosely). I counted the shots played by the straighter of the two — six, not counting the many practice swings, though the contacts of club with ball were fewer; and she had still not reached the road. Upon which, with an impeccably graceful gesture, they stepped aside and waved my partner and myself through. At least they showed every sign of continuing with the round, unlike another transatlantic visitor, who appeared on the tee just in front of a friend of mine, whose word I have no reason to doubt. The American gentleman was splendidly equipped with a bag of clubs and a wife with cine camera. When the time came, he teed up and drove in grand style, every movement being recorded on film by his wife. But then, to my friend's astonishment, he turned to her with the exclamation: 'Right, now for Carnoustie!', then walked from the tee back to Tom Morris's golf shop to return his clubs, hired for the occasion. Another stage in his golfing pilgrimage had been recorded for posterity by his film crew of one.

Quite early one morning, playing golf with my usual Saturday four-ball, I pulled my drive astern of three or four figures ambling up the eighteenth fairway who, in retrospect, I assume to have been more professionally engaged in cinematography. The drive, into the wind, was nothing to boast about; and I was just selecting my three-wood for an optimistic second shot, when over the old bridge came a thick-set, bustling figure, on his way to join the group in front. When he saw me addressing the ball, he considerately paused in his pursuit to wait for me to play. Imagine my embarrassment when, glancing across, I saw it was Lee Trevino. Thinking he would not have found my stroke edifying, I waved him on, advising him not to look. 'That's all right,' he said as he passed; 'but mind the burn, mind the burn!' Then, as an afterthought: 'But you'll not reach the burn.' This I took as an unwarranted slight on my equipment, my appearance or, more probably, my position on the address. Burning with resentment, though to be honest expecting to finish well short of the water, I lashed out in anger at the unsuspecting ball. Taken unawares, it left the club-head with an alacrity such as it never showed before or since and soared over the burn to find a safe haven on the edge of the green. I raised my head, squared my shoulders and looked round with a triumphant smile on my face. But Lee, alas, had already walked on.

On another occasion, my drive had to be postponed because of a gaggle of strollers proceeding this time up my own fairway and evidently returning from the beach. They were quaintly dressed in old-fashioned attire such as is rarely seen today, even on the St Andrews links. I waited until, with mumbled apologies, they regained the footpath beyond the fence. Months later, I was to see them again with a shock of recognition. They were some of the cast of the film *Chariots of Fire*, returning from a shooting session on the West Sands.

At the best of times St Andrews is no place for the short-tempered golfer; and on a sunny summer day the first of his qualities likely to be put to the test on the Old Course is his patience. I think of the apparently interminable stream of folk loitering at five-iron range to or from the sands, parents waiting for lagging toddlers or wayward dogs fresh off the leash, children with rubber rings and their big sisters flaunting the latest thing in beachwear, the occasional string of donkeys quite oblivious to a car or two proceeding at a crawl behind them. Fortunately, the Principal of the University seldom these days exercises his ancient right to spread his washing to dry on the fairway. Still, on an August day such as this, even the straightest of hitters has the problem of his opening drive compounded by the need to calculate the groundspeed of the next approaching group, add a factor for wind speed and direction, and aim accordingly while shouting 'Fore!' as an extra precaution.

Woe betide him if, after all that, he has forgotten to check the make and number of the ball he has just played; for it's then more than likely to come to rest amid a group recently despatched from the eighteenth tee. And after all he's been through, the last thing he wants is to play the wrong ball or have an altercation with a homing golfer eager to give vent to his own pent-up frustrations.

But even stranger things can happen. I recall one sunblest afternoon, when I teed off in a four-ball match, for which our starting time had been reserved. As we were about to hit our drives, we noticed a figure with a bag of clubs scamper across the fairway, obviously heading for the New or Jubilee course, as is often done. At the same time another foursome was driving on the eighteenth. Having played our shots, we walked, chatting together, across the road, when suddenly we noticed not just four balls where we expected ours to be, but a dozen or more, gleaming like unseasonable mushrooms on the turf. Having, with some difficulty, identified our own among the intruders, and seeing the homeward players pass by on their proper station, we realised that the rest must have been shed in his flight by the gentleman who had cut across our own fairway. My partner instinctively gathered up the supernumerary balls, but only to find himself faced with a desperate moral problem. What should we do with them? Take them back to the Starter? But we were already holding up the next match. And there was no time to go in quest of the careless golfer with the unzipped ball pocket. So being a man of total integrity, he resolved to hand them in to the police as lost property; and so I believe he did. I never heard what happened at the station. But I think it's best left to the imagination: 'What's this, then, sir? Golf balls, eh? And where did you come across these? Oh, on the golf course, was it? I see, sir . . .'

However, we're spending too long ourselves on this first hole. So let's get off the green. — Give me that for the half? You're a gentleman, sir!

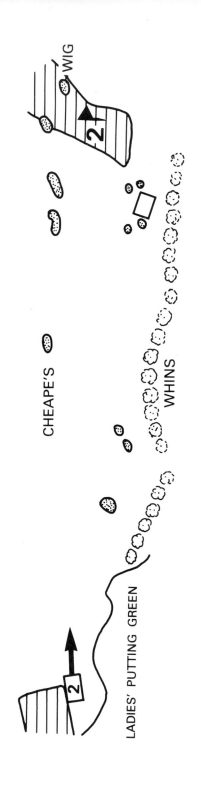

HOLE 2

THE DYKE

YOU CAN RELAX A BIT NOW. MIND YOU, IT'S BEST to keep up appearances as far as possible on the second tee, because you may be under stern scrutiny from one or two of what you take to be that lesser breed putting, apparently for idle enjoyment, on the undulating green to your right. For those are the 'Himalayas', headquarters of the Ladies' Putting Club and the haunt of many an octogenarian beldame who bestrode the links when you were still practising swings in your pram with a rattle. And you'd not want any of them to put the evil eye on you. Once off the tee, though, you should have a screen of whins (gorse) between you and any onlookers to starboard unless, in a fit of relieved exuberance, you hit an impressive slice way over them and find yourself having to ask the occupants of the first tee on the New Course whether they'd been disturbed by any wayward ball. The folk playing the adjacent seventeenth, on your left, should be too far away to notice.

If you're a spasmodic slicer, the Old isn't really the course for you: the New's more accommodating. But I'll try to give you the best direction for straight shots, and it's up to you to compensate as you see fit. So the line to aim for now is over the end of the whins ahead, or just off that low shed to the right of the hotel. It's best not to go too far left, as the wedge of rough between the fairways is very tussocky; and Cheape's bunker is that mound you can see just beyond it. As we're into a stiffish breeze, Cheape's may be out of range; but better safe that sorry. It takes two good shots to reach the green in any case; so like the first, it may be easier to play it as a par five.

Right; the match ahead's well out of range now, and it's still your honour. — That'll do nicely. Now let's see if I can outdrive you. — Damn! I've cut it (only other people slice). That's what comes of trying to hit too hard: more often that not, I fall back off it. Still, I don't think I'm quite far enough over to be in the whins; more likely to be in the humpy rough or one of the little bunkers there. Good resolution for the rest of the round: I must take the club back slowly, keep my eye on the ball, head down and weight forward.

For your next shot, keep out of the rough on the left, where there's a bunker or two. Much safer to the right, as long as you stay clear of the group of traps lurking just off the end of the green. Then you'll have a nice little chip up to the pin. It's on the top level today, where the green's a shallow trough. When it's on the lower end, it's best to aim a little left of the flag, where there's a good chance of the slope bringing the ball round. Mind you, if you're pin high to the right (even on the next tee) you're left with a fairly easy, level putt.

*   *   *

ONE UP TO YOU, THEN, I might still have made the half in five if I hadn't twitched my putt — I shouldn't have played it right-handed. Maybe I'd better confess before we go any further: I'm still struggling a bit with the yips, which inflicted themselves on me a couple of years ago. The worst was in our Spring Meeting, when I excelled myself by getting on the first green in two. By the time I'd holed out in eight, one of my partner's was laughing his head off, the other down on his knees in prayer! I tried everything except a hypnotist. Advice was plentiful and all well-meaning: try a tight grip, slack grip, firm wrists, loose wrists, say to yourself as you line up the two-footer: 'The ball must roll over every little blade of grass, EVERY LITTLE BLADE OF GRASS.' I tried concentrating hard, not concentrating at all, humming *The Blue Danube*, even shutting my eyes, but always with the same result: the ball would either shoot off like a bullet from a rifle when I thought I was still addressing it, or else start demurely on its way only to be given a second rap as the putter head freed itself of all inhibition on the follow-through. Then one day I tried my wife's flat-sided implement back-handed. It was like taking shelter from a hurricane: things are still a bit choppy, but at least *terra firma*'s in sight.

The second tee has its perils. I was once standing there innocently waiting for my turn to drive when like a bolt from the blue a ball caught me plumb on the temple. My partners rushed to render first aid and were surprised to find me still on my feet. The ball's owner quickly arrived with profuse apologies. Playing in the match behind, he'd over-clubbed with a four iron, lost the ball in its flight, then heard a crack and supposed it had hit the tee-box. Though he turned out to be a friend, I still nursed, along with the bruise and the small cut above the eye, the malicious satisfaction of having headed his shot onto the Himalayas out of bounds.

On another occasion, I was among a small gallery of spectators watching the filming of a pro-am tournament featuring Henry Cooper, Britain's favourite heavyweight. Into his golf he put all the mighty aggression shown in his boxing. We were lining the tee like a funnel as he launched into his drive. Though he never pulled his punches, he did have the misfortune to pull this shot. There was a dull thud; and a body dropped to the ground at the end of the funnel. Henry was all concern as the man who had been K.O.'d rose unsteadily to his feet. He was a member of the film crew and had received the shot full on the chest. Fortunately he was wearing a padded anorak; and although he was led away for medical attention, at the end of the day I saw him back with his crew. No doubt he's still earning a drink or two with his story of having once been felled by a left hook from Henry Cooper!

One chill winter day when I had ventured onto the almost deserted course with a friend, we were accosted on this same tee by a Japanese gentleman who had suddenly emerged from behind the whins with a bulky film camera in his hand. Clearly delighted to find somebody actually practising the ancient art at the home of golf, he politely asked if he might record our drives. Preening ourselves a little, we assented and obliged him with what we thought were shots not wholly unworthy of at least a home movie. He thanked us profusely, and then craved one more favour. Turning to my companion (presumably thinking him more photogenic), he asked him if he would mind going to the nearest whin bush and ferret around as if searching for a ball. I should mention that my friend had been a Cambridge blue and, having spent most of his career playing off a minimal handicap, took a certain pride in his game. However, being also a kindly soul, he swallowed that pride and, after only a moment's hesitation, took a club and, albeit unenthusiastically, prodded about in the bush which, being only a few yards off the tee, he had probably never visited before in all his years at St Andrews. Imagine his confusion when, a day or two later, a colleague remarked: 'Saw you on the TV last night — just a short clip from a film the Japanese are making about the Old Course. Didn't have a very good drive on the 2nd, did you?'

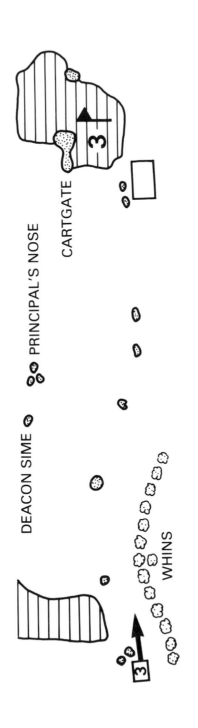

PRINCIPAL'S NOSE

CARTGATE

DEACON SIME

WHINS

HOLE 3

CARTGATE (OUT)

A S YOU CAN SEE, THIS HOLE'S BLIND AND THE line's more or less over the middle of that great rough mound with the bunker in it. You should clear it easily from this tee, though it can pose problems from the medal tee with the wind from the west. — Needless to say, the Old's quite a different course from the tiger tees; but except when they bring one or two of the easier ones into play to give the others a rest, they're strictly for the pros. Straight ahead, then. Too far left towards the fence (that's where the railway line used to run) and you might catch the Principal's Nose. — No, no: it's not his personal proboscis, but a group of three bunkers intended for the drive on the 16th. The Principal himself is rarely seen hereabouts. So stay to the right of the copse you see over there, and you should be in good shape. There's lots of room to the right (the New Course isn't out of bounds at this point, and cross-fraternising is frequent); but there is a line of small bunkers that may well catch a push.

For your second, an iron will probably be enough. It's a difficult shot to judge, because there are a few yards of uneven, raised ground in front of the green, then a small gully, with the large green (shared with the 15th) running away beyond. You'd do well to have a quick look to see where the hole is cut: sometimes it's in a hollow to the back and right, but quite often it's on a narrow plateau in front of the hollow. In general the safer approach is just to the left of the flag, as a running ball is frequently carried away to the right. Don't, though, flirt with Cartgate, the big bunker on the left, where the sand's often hard.

25

IT WAS ON THIS HOLE that many years ago I made, in all innocence, my most unfortunate remark ever on a golf course. My opponent, a doctor, had rejoined me after being called back to attend to a collapsed player on the second tee. 'Let's see,' I said to him, 'isn't this where you have a stroke?'

I also once acted as father confessor here to a young man who had come to play a round on his own, but whom we had invited to make up our four. His swing was majestic, his drives awe-inspiring, and his other shots were of similar quality. A swan among geese, in fact. Yet the look in his eye suggested that he was trying to prove something to himself as well as to us. In our introductory conversations with him (where did he usually play? had he been here before? what was his handicap? and that kind of thing) he had seemed rather evasive; but on this third fairway he finally unburdened his soul to me. That weekend he had played in the final of his club championship (one of the leading Lancashire clubs, if my memory serves). What's more, he was hot favourite to win against an opponent for whom, I gathered, he had little regard. His name was already virtually inscribed in gold letters on the champions' board. Alas, he had played that day the sort of golf that afflicts us all from time to time, and some of us more often than others. He bypassed the grim details of his embarrassing defeat; but soundly beaten he was. Unable to face the derision of his clubmates, he had gone home and looked up the time of the next train to St Andrews 'to get away from it all', he said. The confession patently lightened his burden of guilt; and though I was in no position to offer him absolution, I mentally commended his courage in making it and was delighted to see a first smile light his face, a new spring in his step, and a few shots casual and loose enough to put us all in good humour.

It was on this same fairway that one of my companions, a cheerfully wild hitter of the ball, had a most vicious shank with one of his longer irons. As this was by no means an uncommon feat for him, it was extremely imprudent of another member of our group to have walked on a few yards and paused at what in cricket parlance would be called short extra cover. There he stood, with his four iron in his hand, waiting to play his own shot. With startling velocity the shanked ball struck the iron plumb on the steel shaft, in which, to our amazement, it left a small dent. Fortunately, no other damage was done to man or equipment; and we went happily and with a certain relief on our way. But that's only half the story. Remind me to tell you the rest on the seventeenth, if we're still on speaking terms then.

Yes, that was a difficult spot for the pin. You can't be blamed for three-putting from the bottom of that bank. Still, that's back to all square.

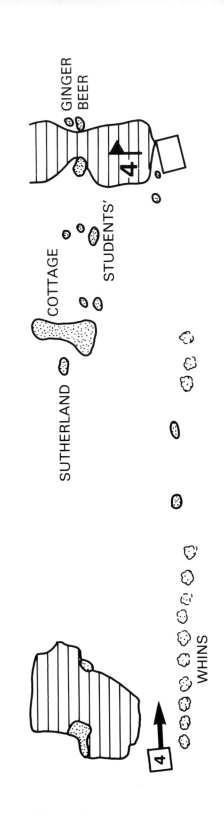

GINGER BEER

COTTAGE

STUDENTS'

SUTHERLAND

WHINS

HOLE 4

GINGER BEER

THE HOLE'S BEEN SO NAMED FOR OVER A century and a half because it used to be a place where golfers would slake their thirst with that beverage (somewhat fortified, no doubt), provided by a local worthy from his handcart. The course followed a different route in those days, which accounts for the unlikely siting of the refreshments. But at least they were available then, which is not the case today — unless, that is, you're concealing a flask of something behind that bulge in your bag.

This is another longish one, and there are two recognised routes to the green (you can just see the flag at the end of what looks like a valley from here). If you're a straight hitter, you'll not go far wrong by driving up that valley; but if you think you can get the length to land on top of the bank towards the fifteenth fairway (no further left than the tiled roof you can see), that will give you a lie on or over the plateau and a better sight of the green. It's certainly the preferable line when the hole is cut to the left; otherwise you're liable to have to approach it over that small hump you can just make out in front of the green. But either way, if you feel a slice coming on, you'd better use a crossed finger grip: to the right of the valley and you might catch one of a couple of bunkers or even land in thickish rough towards the second hole on the New; and if you slice off the left-hand line, you're likely to finish among the humps and hollows you can see.

I think I'll try to go to the left. — Oh dear, I fell off it again. Ah, what a bit of luck! I've just kicked off the nose of that bank onto the fairway. — Good shot: you've got there the honest way. Now you have a straight approach to the

29

pin, which is to the right of the hummock today. It looks as though it's fairly well back, so don't underclub: this green's very deep, and it has a bit of a ridge in the middle. Another thing is you'll usually have an easier putt from the right — probably uphill and with fewer borrows. But whatever you do, don't get among the rough bumps and bushes to the right of the fairway: that's desperate country, although it ends well short of the green.

That's fine: you should get your par all right from there. Anyway, a five's no disgrace on this one. It was from this tee, though, that I once came as near as ever I've been to a hole in one. Yes, you've guessed it: a drive off the heel onto the fifteenth green. And I can still remember the reaction of the people putting out there. But they were quite nice about it once the shock had worn off. It was there too that my younger son, before he even aspired to a handicap, began an interesting run of 6, 5, 4, 3, 2.

It's strange how your scores can sometimes take on a perverse life of their own. From what you've seen so far, you'll gather that I'm one of the world's dullest players. On one occasion on the New I took five at every hole up to the seventeenth, which was fairly typical of my golf in an exaggerated sort of way. So you can imagine the surprise of my partners as well as myself when, in a competition a couple of years ago, my figures from this hole to the twelfth inclusive contained one 8, two 7s, a 6, a 5, a 4, two 3s and a 2 — which, of course, works out at level fives!

* * *

THE MOST DRAMATIC BIRDIE I'VE SEEN was achieved from the fourth tee — by the friend, in fact, whose shaft was dented on the third, as I told you. Like Henry Cooper, he tends to give his shots everything he's got, which in this case turned out to be more than sufficient for the result achieved. Away soared the ball at the very moment when, fifty yards ahead, a warbling lark was engaged in its own carefree soar, vertically, in the spring sunshine. The trajectories of ball and bird, alas, intersected; and to our dismay we saw that 'blithe spirit' plummet, like an old-time 'feathery', into the heather ahead. Steeling ourselves, we went to perform the last rites; but no bird was there — flown, we devoutly hoped, if not retired to nurse a sore head in its nest. It's uncanny how now, when my friend (we'll call him D.D. for later identification) takes a club in his hand, every lark in the vicinity seems to stop singing.

It must have been on one of the practice days before the 1970 Open here that I took my two sons out on the course to watch some of the players practising (in those days, no one had thought of charging for the privilege). We had reached this hole, having helped one of the lesser lights look for his ball in the rough, when someone said Jack Nicklaus was out at the loop. 'Come on,' I said: 'there's nothing much happening here, so let's go out to the turn.' This was not to the liking of David, the elder boy. So, having spotted a couple of players on the fifteenth tee, he decided to stroll across and give them the benefit of a gallery of one, while John and I went on in search of bigger game in the shape of the Golden Bear. The two loners, we were later proudly informed, were quite happy to have the company. 'Hullo,' said one of them. 'What's your name?' — 'David. What's yours?' — 'I'm Tom Shaw, and this is . . .' To my shame, I forget the other name. Anyway, it appears that a passing friendship was struck up, with the result that on the day of the opening round, David was determined to go out by the first green to watch 'my friend Tom Shaw' open his challenge; and so it was. The hero duly appeared, and with a couple of well-aimed strokes was on the green, above the pin. He was left with a long putt for his birdie. Suddenly, disaster! Deceived by the speed of the green and perhaps by a following breeze, he watched his ball run past the hole, and on and on, finally to trickle off the green and down into the Swilcan Burn. But then, before the admiring gaze of David, his hero leapt the burn and, having taken a penalty drop on

31

the further side, calmly holed his chip back. David had seen enough. He returned home at once so that no other memories should dim that radiant moment.

What's that? Your hole? — Oh, yes, I suppose it was. I must have been talking too much. But now for one of the two long ones, so I'd better pull myself together. No, I don't think you'll find it too daunting, although most of the holes, as I've said, are quite a different proposition from the tiger tees. I've only played the whole course from them a couple of times: *after* a championship, I hasten to add. Just look out for them as we go round, and you'll see that from one or two it takes quite a long drive just to reach the fairway. Into the wind it can be a most humbling experience; but at least we'll not be tested that way today.

Over to the fifth tee, then, and your honour.

B

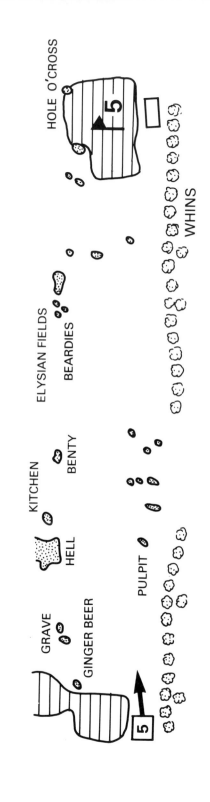

HOLE O'CROSS
(OUT)

YOU SEE THOSE TWO BUNKERS ON THE HILL IN the distance? No, you'll not drive them, though it has been done! What I was going to say is that your line's no further right than the left-hand one. As usual, the golden rule is keep over to the left side of the fairway. The reason here is that there's a line of bunkers on driving length to the right of the direct line to the pin. The first one's called Pulpit; and I've heard many an unholy sermon preached from there, I can assure you. As with most of the bunkers on the Old, you're unlikely to get far out of the sand, so if Fate (or one's usual desperately bad luck!) takes you there, you have to resign yourself to a lost shot. Yes, that's fine — oh, 'FORE!' It's all right; you're well short of him. No, he hasn't suddenly materialised: he's playing the other way and is perfectly entitled to use our fairway — in fact it's the best route to the fourteenth, as you'll discover. You may think you're taking your life in your hands every time you play on this course; but the annual fatality rate is really surprisingly low.

So here we are, both more or less down the middle, but without any chance of reaching the putting surface. What you can't see from here is that over that bank ahead is a deep gully running across in front of the green — which, by the way, is shared with the thirteenth and is one of the biggest in golf. I dare say a flight of helicopters could land on it in formation, so long as they squared it with the Joint Links Committee! It's not the easiest green to miss; but should you achieve that feat, there's a great basin of heather to the left of the left-hand bunker and a good selection of humps and hollows and long grass over the one on the right. You have to have a sure aim to go between them; so I won't think you a coward if you play short and leave yourself an easy pitch over the gully to the green. That's reasonably flat; but I suggest a quick reconnaissance up the nearest bank to see where the hole's cut. Pride can so easily turn to dismay when you find you've left yourself a forty-yard putt. And no chipping on the green, please (though it's occasionally done in championships)!

That'll do fine! You're a hard man to follow, but here goes! I'll aim for the bunker on the left to allow for my fade. Ah, that's better: off the middle for a change. Oh, no! Not into it! What a moment to conquer my slice — I mean fade, Three . . . four . . . five . . . six — too late to play out backwards now, so I'll just pick up. That bunker's impossible. If you have to go in one, it's best to choose the other. Yes, you go ahead and putt out. I'll just get the sand out of my hair and join you on the next tee.

*　　*　　*

I CAN TELL YOU NOW that I once found a spent .303 bullet by that bunker. There was no sign of the corpse, so I can only suppose it had been tactfully removed. It's amazing how seriously some people take the game. But how else could you account for it? Even the most fiery R. and A. colonel would normally leave his armaments in the clubhouse; but I can imagine some swaggering fellow tucking his revolver into his bag, having vowed over his whisky: 'If ever I fail to get out of a bunker in one, I swear to you I'll . . .' Or perhaps it was another failed club champion. But we'll never know: these things tend to get hushed up in St Andrews.

Talking of the R. and A., every year, during their Autumn Meeting, they challenge the town clubs to a match over the Old, and a very convivial occasion it is. As a member of the opposition, one goes with one's partner to the first tee to come face to face with the designated foemen, whose names one has already seen on a list, but forgotten. Introductions are brief and informal: 'I'm Bill, he's John' kind of thing. One may or may not glean further information about them in the course of the round; but failing that, the leather armchairs and silver flagons in the Big Room after the game encourage confidences. I would be loath to accuse any of these gentleman golfers of premeditated gamesmanship, at least none of those outside my own circle of acquaintances; and I'm sure what happened once in the middle of the fifth fairway was not deliberately contrived to unnerve the humble challengers. Be that as it may, we were much taken aback when Bill (or was it John?) hit one of his better balls, and with a roar that must have caused all the golfers on the adjacent fairways to duck, his partner gave full expression to his admiration: 'Good shot AMBASSADOR!' Having recovered my poise by the time we reached the green, I found it hard to refrain from complimenting my own partner with a cry of: 'Fine putt, your Grace!'

Some years ago, I was asked if I would guide a visiting American round the course, and took little persuading. I met him at the first tee: a brisk, charming man, who carried his own clubs as to the manner born and wasted no time in putting them to good, if rather wayward, use. It was another case of playing with him first and learning his identity later. I'm glad I did, for I was subsequently able to use the knowledge in my one and only letter to *The Times*. It was in reply to their report of a licence granted for onshore oil and gas exploration in an area 'which includes the Royal and Ancient golf course at St Andrews'. After putting them right over their terminology, I was able to assure them that, having myself operated over the links for many years and excavated to a considerable depth in the process, I had struck about everything but oil. And remembering my American acquaintance and that one enjoyable round, I felt it helpful to add that I had visited most parts of the Old Course with the President of one of the major oil corporations, who had given no hint of discovering anything more significant than a rather battered ball in the gorse on the fifth hole. The present absence of oil rigs, even on the fifth green, which would be an obvious site, suggests that my inside information did not go unheeded.

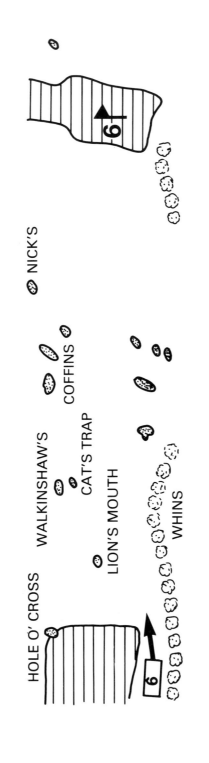

HOLE O' CROSS

WALKINSHAW'S

COFFINS

NICK'S

CAT'S TRAP

LION'S MOUTH

WHINS

HOLE 6

HEATHERY (OUT)

T HIS IS THE ONLY HOLE WITH A DIRECTION POST, albeit a modest and cringing thing. The reason for it is obvious, although its usefulness is questionable. The first thing to do in any case is to walk on a few yards until you can see whether it's safe to proceed. Not only will you often find players still hunting for their balls, but folk from the thirteenth may well have taken an option on this fairway for reasons we'll come to. Yes, from here the hole does look straightforward enough; but just come back to the tee, and we'll look from there.

The problem is that if you hit your shot over the post and have even a slight fade, you're quite likely to be drawn round into one of five bunkers at the right edge of the fairway. That's bad enough; but slice into a head wind and you may well finish in the whins to the right of that. It's by no means unknown for players putting on the fourth green of the New Course to have an unexpected visit from here. No, even that's not out of bounds. Where do you aim, then? Well, certainly left of the post. The hangars at Leuchars airfield are a favourite mark; or even the quarry you can see on the hill to the left of that. Don't overdo it, though, because there are a few traps between the two fairways and on the length of a good drive. They're called the Coffins; and I wouldn't like to see you laid out in one of them. Grisly sense of humour? Yes, I agree. But that's what happens the more you play round here: your sense of humour gets blackened and stunted like the few trees that survive the natural rigours of the links.

You can drive, then. There should be no difficulty in getting over all the rough hillocks from here. But from the

41

back tees you certainly need a clean hit, or even a mighty slog against the wind; and in those conditions it's best to go for the left-hand end of the bank.

Nice shot! But don't look too pleased with yourself until you see where you've finished: you started a bit close to the post, and the ball was drifting a little at the end. Oh, and I've gone too far the other way. I'll see you at the green, then. It's one of the truer ones; just make sure you get right up, as the front begins in a shallow valley just over the ridge. There are no bunkers to worry about near the green, just the critical eyes of that expert-looking group on the tee. If you push your shot, you could find yourself putting from under their noses.

*　　*　　*

WHENEVER I STAND ON THE SIXTH TEE and look at that shelter near the whins beside it, I remember a remarkable scene I once watched from there on a bright but blustery day one Easter. My group was waiting to drive, without paying too much attention to the large black cloud looming up at our backs — in any case, it's remarkable how often storms, with proper deference, skirt these links and pass them by. But not this time. A large white, downy object came floating down the wind, then another, and another; and soon the air was full of them, as if all the chickens in the celestial kitchens were being plucked for an Easter celebration. We made a dash for that shelter and watched with dismay while the snow fell ever thicker. Our refuge soon became overcrowded as the minutes ticked by. The blizzard was as intense as I'd ever seen in these parts; and still it went on. When it eased a little, we found that a white blanket had been drawn over the courses; and it soon became obvious that it would be impossible for us to continue our round. After a while, the sky brightened again; and as it did so, small groups of hunched figures appeared from whatever shelter they had taken, all plodding in the same direction — back towards the distant grey line of the town. It was a scene such as one of those old Dutch masters might have painted; or rather, as I thought at the time, like a shot from a Cecil B. de Mille screen epic. Napoleon's retreat from Moscow sprang to mind, as we joined the fleeing rabble. At least we hadn't driven off, unlike most of the others, who had no choice but to leave their ammunition scattered over the course where it lay, completely covered by the snow. You can imagine how much that must have hurt in this part of the world! I've often thought, though, that once the thaw came, the local ball-hunters would have had a rich harvest for the reaping. It's an ill wind . . .

Did you notice that furtive figure with the dog, prodding around in the whins as you came down the fairway? He's one of that confraternity who hope to turn over an honest penny or two by taking advantage of the golfers' more extravagant moments (though technically, I'm told, they're not supposed to operate before sundown). The dog and stick are vital parts of their equipment; and I've no doubt that a hound with a good nose for a Dunlop 65 or Titleist is much prized in their circles. I was once told of an owner who, seeing his own hairy companion with a pronounced hangdog expression on its face, went over to investigate and found its eyes riveted on a round white

object under a whin. It was only when the dog disobeyed the usual instruction to 'fetch' that he discovered its maw already full to bursting with five other balls. This group of whins has a voracious appetite and a far better digestive system than the dog, as was shown when quite recently one of the ancient 'feathery' balls was discovered hereabouts, still nursing its old battle-wounds.

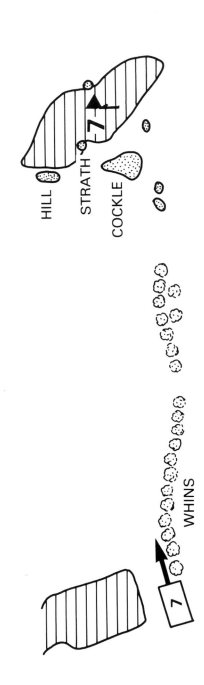

HILL

STRATH

COCKLE

WHINS

7

7

HIGH (OUT)

I THINK I SCRAPED THAT, DIDN'T I? SO IT'S BACK
to one. Now for one of the more tricky holes.

It's a slight dog-leg right, so we can't quite see the pin
from here: it's more or less behind the end of the furthest
whins. The driving line (unless you can hit a really big one)
is for the red flag on the 11th green; in other words to the
right-hand end of the hill you see ahead. Failing that, the
left-hand line's the safer. To the right is what my usual four-
ball knows as 'Harry's Hollow': the term dates back to the
time before that exponent of the art had cured a persistent
slice and was too optimistic to allow for it (he's now a
reformed character and rather sensitive on the subject). It's
a deep depression with a couple of bushes and can make the
next shot problematical. To the left of the hill and a little
way past it is a large bunker nicknamed 'the Admiral's' for
reasons I'll divulge later. But that's probably out of range
for us, a more immediate inconvenience being that clump of
grass you see ahead, round one of the ancient boundary
stones. Miss that, and you're likely to find yourself at the
bottom of, or part of the way up, the hill itself. From there
(the most common destination of my drives) it's possible to
reach the green with a mid-iron and a bit of luck, after a
judicious reconnaissance.

Let's have a go, then! Ah, as usual! — Oh, you're
really well left; but no damage has been done. From where
you are you may have a direct second shot without needing
to carry any bunkers. Yes, there you are. It's a tight line all
right; but if you're straight, a topped runner can still make
the green. I, on the other hand, will have to try and drop my
ball just over Cockle: that's the great excavation in front of

47

the green. Officially it's a bunker, though it seldom contains much identifiable sand, except under the face. One mustn't be too caustic, though, because with all the wind we get round here it would be impossible to keep fine sand in some of the traps unless they were roofed over — and that's not a bad idea, come to think of it. The result here is that, unless you're close to the face, you can play a fairly orthodox wedge shot to the pin, taking care to avoid a little deep bunker called the Kidney, I think, which lurks just over the right-hand corner of Cockle.

Me to go? I'd better just check there's no one on the fairway; the eleventh crosses our hole at this point, and homeward players have the right of way — which means it's our insurance that would have to pay for any injury! Oh dear! I hit that rather too sweetly, and it's gone some way up the rough hill behind the green. That may well spell disaster, as my short shots (rudely referred to by my ex-friends as 'twitch and runs') deserted me like my putting, but rather earlier. I thought I'd cured them a month or two back — by swinging with virtually the left arm only. That actually worked for a whole practice round. But then, back to the twitch, only more so. Any tips?

Here's one for you. The green slopes fairly sharply all the way down from the eleventh, so you'll usually find a shot well left of the pin will grope its way across towards the hole. Mind you don't get into Strath, though; that's the small bunker guarding the green to the left of Cockle. Although it's one that does keep its sand, it doesn't take kindly to a visitor from the seventh hole.

*   *   *

THE TEE WE'VE JUST LEFT is one of the more sheltered ones, which is just as well when the course is crowded, as it's also one where hold-ups can occur. — No, no: I mean you may have to wait for a while, with nothing in peril but the rhythm you were trying to convince yourself that you'd just found. The delay may be caused partly by players ahead rummaging in 'Harry's Hollow' or the more sinister patches of whin, partly by others waiting for the green to clear, and partly by the traffic passing in leisurely fashion from eleventh tee to green. So you'd be wise to keep a few scraps of conversation for offering round here, rather like the Kendal mint cake or Moffat toffee at the turn.

The point was brought home to a friend when, after curbing his impatience for some minutes while waiting for the group of ladies ahead to move on, he was relieved to see them stop their animated discussion and walk over to their balls. All except one. She suddenly clapped her hand to her head, turned on her heel, and hurried back to the tee, driver in hand. 'I'm terribly sorry,' she said on arrival: 'do you mind if I play before you? The thing is I was talking so much, I forgot to drive with my friends.'

An experience of my own was not dissimilar. We had been limping along behind a foursome of enthusiastic but somewhat wayward transatlantic visitors. One lady was particularly unpredictable, as we'd had occasion to observe. Now the whole party, having played their second shots, had followed her into the whins to conduct what I used to know from my erstwhile navigational training as a 'creeping line ahead' search. Eventually they waved to us to go through, which we proceeded to do. Walking to my own ball, I passed another, which I assumed must have fallen from one of the party's bags. When I called across to make sure, the errant member asked its make and number. I told her. 'Oh gee,' she cried in delight, 'that's mine: I never could have guessed it would be on the fairway!'

For the sake of my conscience, I feel bound to tell of another incident on this hole. Playing in one of the major club competitions, I was up that hill doing my usual reconnaisance when I noticed considerable activity in the big bunker on the left. It was a fellow-competitor who was repeatedly bending and then hurling one stone after another from the sand. Now my working knowledge of the rules of golf extended to the fact that loose impediments in hazards were not to be removed; and I had once even penalised myself for pocketing a tee I found in one. So I thought the blackest thoughts, which were no whit lightened when I saw his name high on the results list. For years I nursed my resentment, thinking myself charitable for not having him drummed out of the club. Until, that is, the day when, during one of those hiatuses in play, I casually turned my card over and read the Local Rules on the back. Yes, you've guessed. 'Stones in bunkers are movable obstructions.' So when the presumed offender was proposed for Club Captain, I raised no objections. I really must make a point of reading backs of scorecards more often.

Well, I was lucky to scramble a half there. Come on, let's see if I can square things on the next. That's the beginning of the so-called loop, which comprises the next four holes and can sometimes bolster a sagging morale.

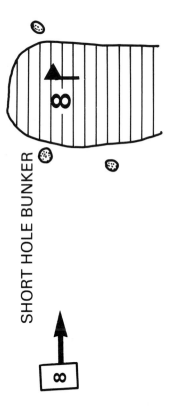

SHORT HOLE BUNKER

8

SHORT HOLE

YOU MIGHT THINK THAT THIS IS A TIGER TEE back here on the hill; but in fact it's a fairly recent addition to save those on the flat from too much wear and tear. This means that, depending on conditions and the tee in play, you may need anything from a modest 8-iron to a full-blooded drive. If the latter, beware the scattering of whins to the left. Going that way (by accident, not design) you need both a good carry and a lungful of air ready for a shout of 'Fore!' to any unsuspecting group with their backs turned on the next teeing ground. The hazard to the right is obvious: that great rough depression, at the back of which lurks a bunker. The fact that it's rarely visited makes it even more of a surprise when you rediscover it. The one that advertises its presence, of course, is the sandy cavity set in the hillock in front of the green. As today, the pin is very often placed directly behind it. The difficulty from here is to see just how far, as the green is quite deep. From the lower tees, if you carry the bunker by three or four yards, you should be all right; but with a long club from here, it might be touch and go. The green itself does slope up from the front at that point, so you could hold it; but it's safer to play to the side of the trap. Although you may have some tricky borrows to negotiate, you can afford to breathe out once you're on the putting surface.

Have a go, then; just to the right of the bunker would be ideal. Oh, it's my honour, is it? — Well, not exactly as intended, but it'll do. — Ah, you may have come off that one a bit. Just as well it's a double green! One advantage is that it gives you a close-up view of the positioning of the tenth flag; and you'll find that very useful when we play the hole. I'm usually too preoccupied to look, and then regret the omission later.

* * *

FOR SOME REASON, this hole seems to inspire the more erratic shot. One member of my usual group came to it once rather shaken by a prolonged bout of activity in Cockle while playing the seventh. This tee was at the bottom that day, and the wind from the east. Gritting his teeth and determined to make amends for his recent aberration, he attacked the ball with all the concentration he could muster. The result was one of the most spectacular shanks you could wish to see someone else play, with the ball looping away to the right and then, encouraged by the wind, dropping at about ninety degrees to the line of aim — straight into Cockle!

Every morning when I brush my teeth, I close my eyes to avoid seeing that sinister imprint on the basin: 'SHANKS'. Do people of that name, I wonder, ever take up the game? That surely would be to tempt providence. And though I joined in the general hilarity at my friend's embarrassment, my mirth was tempered by the thought that, but for the grace of the gods of golf, there might I have gone. I say that advisedly because, though my shanks these days are fairly rare (except, of course, when I tell myself it would be fatal to do one at that moment), there was one occasion when I more or less shanked my way round the whole loop. My opponent, a true gentleman, was so concerned that he told me of his own past lapses in that respect and how a professional had given him the infallible cure. On the address, he said, I should keep my arms as close as possible to my body and feel them brush against my jacket on the backswing: that's all. I tried it; and to my delight it worked. We continued the round; and all went smoothly until the sixteenth hole, where an intended

54

approach shot skewed the ball viciously out of bounds. But the shot was his! And he followed that up with two further shanks on the seventeenth. Poor man! He has, I think, since recovered; but whether he still proffers his helpful advice on the subject I doubt. Part of the irony is that it did help me, and I'm still indebted to him for it.

Another strange sight I have enjoyed (if that's the word) from the eighth tee was of a foursome armed with putters but indulging in a kind of slow-motion sword dance. It must, I thought, be some sort of midsummer ritual imported from foreign parts. Then I noticed that one of the participants had a cine camera, and all became clear. Suddenly, they noticed that they were holding us up; and in a trice they left the green and waved cheerfully for us to play. This we did. But no sooner had our shots come to rest than they all were back on the green, but putting out this time. Our arrival anticipated the consummation of that part of the ceremony, so they stood aside once more, but now with the camera trained on us. We made good speed to the next tee, I can assure you. And that's where we'll go now.

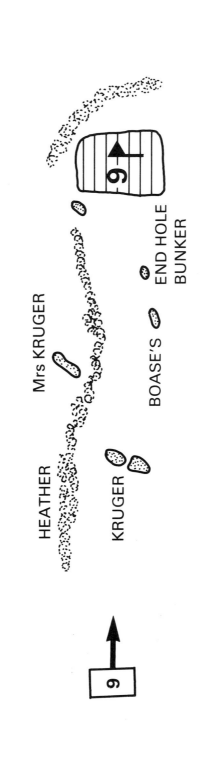

HEATHER

Mrs KRUGER

KRUGER

BOASE'S

END HOLE
BUNKER

9

HOLE 9

END HOLE

THIS SHOULD, I SUPPOSE, BE IN NORMAL conditions the easiest of the par fours. The fairway and green, though, are so flat and featureless that judgment of distance becomes the most difficult aspect. I have to admit that, to my shame no doubt, I've never bothered with working out yardages (are they called metrages these days?), and for two very good reasons. The first is that I've never known how far I can expect to hit the ball with my various clubs: so much depends on whether I slice it, hook it, thin it, skin it, sclaff it, shank it, smother it, get it off the toe or off the heel, get under it, top it, come off it, fall over it, or now and then give it a good clip. The second, and less personal, reason is that meteorological conditions are so unstable in St Andrews, what with sudden wind and temperature changes, the coming and going of the haar (sea fog) and so forth, that the length and characteristics of the holes change as though they were on a piece of elastic. I know that this admission will have sunk me in your estimation; but the truth will out.

The main thing here is to put your drive somewhere on the fairway, but for once you don't need to be too choosy. You see our path to the right of this rough bank? Well there are a couple of bunkers, called Kruger, on either side, about where it joins the fairway; but you shouldn't normally be troubled by them. What you can't see from here is that beyond and to the left of the path is a heathery waste and set in it another bunker of ample proportions, unflatteringly called Mrs Kruger. So stick to the right of that. If you're like me, you'll aim at Boase's bunker in the middle of the fairway, on the assumption that you're unlikely to hit one absolutely straight. Should your pride not allow that, then

57

there's a good deal of room to the left of it and, for once, even more to the right. From anywhere on the fairway, the second shot's straightforward to that dully (or do I mean delightfully?) flat green. A really good drive (the green's just about in range in favourable conditions) might get you into that small pot beyond Boase's, which in my case would be a cause as much for satisfaction as regret; and after a monstrous pull you might even find yourself in a bunker near the whins off the left-hand corner of the green. However, as I'd played the course for a number of years before I even discovered that one, you hardly need to worry about it now.

HOLE 9 : END HOLE

I'M GLAD TO FIND the tee box is intact. Once, as we were putting out on the eighth, with no other golfers in sight, we looked across and saw smoke issuing from it. By the time we'd reached it, it was well and truly alight — that too could have been part of some midsummer ritual, though we were alone in dancing round it, until the conflagration was extinguished. A more mundane explanation, I fancy, was a smouldering cigarette end that had finally ignited the rubbish which, fanned by the wind, had produced the spectacular blaze we had to quench. Even so, one mystery remained: why should the 'rubbish' in question have been not empty wrappings or torn-up scorecards, but a discarded pair of trousers? — Any suggestions?

The suddenness with which conditions can change, even on a clear day, was illustrated one summer evening when we had been playing blessed by a warm zephyr and in shirt sleeves, until we came to this tee. Before we left it, there had been an abrupt transformation; the breeze had swung round to the east and, though not strong, had produced a chill that quickly made us don jerseys and jackets.

The only time I've ever found a full set of clubs on a course was under a bush over there to the left. There being not a player in sight, not even 'claiming relief' among the whins, I spent a few perplexed minutes wondering what to do with them. Eventually, to my own relief, a figure appeared running across from the sixth tee of the New Course, beyond the whins on the other side of the fairway. If I disentangled his story properly from between the pants, I had arrived to witness the end of a very heroic act. One of his party having been taken ill on the tee, he had decided to head for the West Sands road, running across three courses and dropping his clubs as he went. Finding no phone or immediate transport there, he had to continue a good way towards the town before enrolling the necessary help. I'm not sure whether he intended to complete his round.

This hole was also the scene of another gallant, though

less humanitarian act. I was playing one day with those two eminent gentlemen I mentioned when we were on the first hole. Two of us drove to our satisfaction, but the third, a philosopher, sent his ball bounding with considerable impetus into Boase's bunker. There was no doubt about it: we'd all seen it go in. He went to play it; but of the ball there was no sign. The bunker must recently have been replenished, as it was then full of soft sand, such as I've not seen for many a year. The philosopher pushed and prodded with his club, devoting a good deal of logic, if not metaphysics, to the operation; but search as he might, he had to abandon his efforts and move on. I saw him the following day. — 'I got that ball, by the way.' — 'Not the one in the bunker?' — 'Yes. I cycled out there last night with a rake.' Knowing my friend, it was unlikely to have been a new ball!

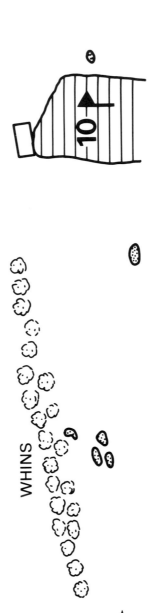

WHINS

10

HOLE 10

(No Name)

SO THIS IS THE TURN, AND YOU'RE STILL ONE UP
after that half in par (you did three-putt like me on the
short hole, didn't you?). You're out in 44, I think. Not bad
for your first time on the Old: perhaps I should leave you to
find your own way around. By the way, there's a tap over
there, if you're thirsty. — Oh, so there was something
significant behind that bulge in your bag. I should take up
whisky divining! Well, only a small tot, thanks, just to settle
the nerves and steel the resolve. This brings out the bard in
me, so here's a parody (only a slight one) of an old Scottish
poet:

> The rule of these links is a paradox quite,
> Both in driving and playing along:
> If you keep to the left, you are sure to be right,
> If you keep to the right, you are wrong.

He can't have been thinking of this hole, though, for
it's one of the few (like its partner the ninth) where it pays to
keep right: you can see the line of heather to the left, and
tough stuff it is. At its edge, and quite short, is a pair of
small back-to-back bunkers to catch a topped drive; but I
insult you to suggest that they are a problem. More
dangerous is that one you can see on the length of a good
drive, although with a decent lie you should make the green
from it. Yes, it is one of the shorter par fours: only about
twenty yards longer than the ninth and also drivable by the
long hitters: in my case, though, it would take rather more
than one wee dram! — No, that wasn't a hint, thanks all the
same.

When you reach the green, you'll find a few tantalising

slopes, rather like those on the eighth. The hole, as we saw, is fairly well back today, so you should be able to pitch over the low bank in front of it. Not too far beyond, though, because the green does slope away over there, and you don't want to be through.

* * *

AH, THAT WAS ONE OF MY BETTER DRIVES, thanks to the spirit you instilled into me. You're rather far right. That doesn't matter, so long as you keep an eye on those people getting ready to drive on the ninth tee. I don't know what the Japanese for 'Fore!' is, do you? I'm sure they would apologise most charmingly, but that's not much consolation for a cracked rib.

One of my usual partners, preferring to save as much energy as possible for his shot-making, has the habit of leaving his bag of clubs, less the putter and driver, where his drive finished on the ninth, and picking them up again on his way to this green. None of us has as yet managed to hit our drive into the inviting mouth of the bag, though it's sure to happen some time. On the other hand, he has been known more than once to force a bit from the tee, get one about twenty yards off the heel, and find he has to play the next shot from thick rough behind a whin bush with either a driver or a putter.

There's really no point in trying too hard for length on a hole like this. I remember once having to play a past club champion, receiving plenty of strokes of course. He'd been badly off his putting, and I was a hole or so up as we started the loop. When he launched a majestic shot off the ninth tee, I was put in mind of the Old Testament: 'The driving is like the driving of Jehu . . . for he driveth furiously.' Unfortunately for him, he had pulled the shot slightly, and the ball disappeared into the furthest whins, never to be seen again. Then on this hole, having taken another shining victim from its wrappings, he punished it just like the first; and off it sped to seek sanctuary in the bushes to the left of this green.

We all know well enough that rhythm is more important than sheer power at this game. I once had an interesting conversation with a non-golfing cellist and was amazed to find how much the essentials of the two activities had in common, beginning with the 'stance', including head position, and details like grooving the swing (you're not a cellist, I hope?), but above all the maintenance of timing and rhythm. More recently, I had the chance of speaking to an exponent of the double bass, who had fortunately been on hand to help out in a concert when one member of the scheduled group had been taken ill. And how did he happen to be in St Andrews? Why, he'd come to fulfil his ambition of playing the Old Course, on his way to an engagement further north. He confirmed all I had learned from the cellist. Then I asked what for me was the crucial question: can one get the yips on the double bass? Oh yes, he assured me: it's a common occurrence, and notoriously so when the music is a particular piece of Mahler. He went on to insist that there is one infallible cure: the so-called Alexander technique for developing correct posture, centred on keeping the neck and spine straight. I suspect there's something in it; but I have still to master the residual problem of hitting the putt straight while my eyes are fixed on the distant horizon.

Now let's see what I can do with this one. Damn, that's pushed! Oh, sorry! It must have come in off a spike mark. Still, I'm not too proud to accept it for a par; and as they always say, it's not how but how many. And yours jinked the other way. Bad luck! It must have been in my horoscope that I was to go all square here.

c

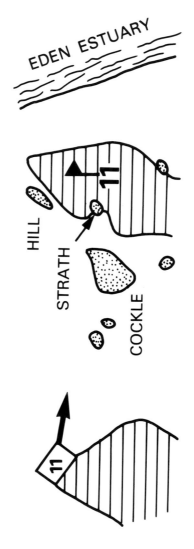

EDEN ESTUARY

HILL

STRATH

COCKLE

HOLE 11

H IGH (IN)

I SEE THE NEXT TEE'S UP ON THE HILL: THE MEDAL and championship ones are always down here on the flat. Still, we get a better view of the hole from up there — not that it's a reassuring prospect.

The perils are more or less visible: the whins at our feet for a complete duff; the Cockle for a short one off the nose, Hill (that's the monster to the left of the green) for a pull; Strath on the other side for a fade (that's a very friendly one, as it gathers you in with open arms and is reluctant to let you go); then there's a steep drop over the back, with long grass not far beyond and the estuary beyond that should you badly over-club. As you can see, the green slopes down from behind the hole; so you can imagine the difficulty, should you go through it, of pitching back and holding.   Strath will always be delighted to receive you, even if you had given it the cold shoulder and not dropped in on your way from the tee. Why do you suppose they usually cut the hole, as today, right behind it? Pure sadism. — What's that? No, of course this isn't gamesmanship. I'm simply rehearsing my own excuses.

Let's see: I think I'll take a four wood today into this breeze. — Well, that's not too bad, if it keeps out of Hill. A bit long, though. Will it hold? Just, I fancy: somewhere near the high tee. Now let's see what you can do. Better short than long, then, as long as you're straight. You can always putt up from the foot of the green. A quick prayer might not come amiss. — Weren't you a bit tentative? And you did fall off it a little. But at least you're over Cockle; just on the green, I think, though that's not particularly good news. — I do hope I didn't put you off. — Why isn't it good news?

67

You'll see when you get there; but unless I'm mistaken, you'll find that friendly Strath's right on the line of your putt, if you can hit it that far. You may have prayed for grace to put your ball on the green; but in St Andrews you have to be much more precise in your supplications. Now you'll have to aim for the top of the green and hope for a nice roll down towards the pin.

*   *   *

IT WAS TOO KIND OF YOU to give me that two-footer. But you've broken one of the golden rules of St Andrews golf, which is never to concede a putt on the eleventh (quite apart from the fact that it puts me one up). Not only is there all this slope, but the green gets polished by the wind and is usually very fast. In fact you did quite well yourself to get down in three from where you were. And as for your tee shot, I've seen far worse. I vividly remember, for instance, watching this hole during one of the major championships (the inaugural Eisenhower Trophy in 1958, I think), when there was half a gale blowing from the west. One competitor easily outbid you by hitting such a handsome slice that his ball finished a few feet away from the seventh pin. I didn't count his putts.

I was only watching then; but more recently I had to operate myself in even more stormy conditions. I say 'had to' because it was in a club match-play competition, and my opponent had come over from Edinburgh on the last day available for the tie. You can judge the strength of the wind by the fact that he told me there were speed restrictions on the motorway when he came over. Indeed I learned later that even the caddies, battered and exhausted by services rendered in the morning, had refused to go out in the afternoon. A party of visitors, on the first tee ahead of us, were virtually blown back to the Starter's box, and insisted that we took their place. So we struggled round until we reached the eleventh where, after an unspecified number of shots, we arrived on the green below the hole, which was placed well up the bank. First one of us then the other hit our balls towards the hole, only to see them, having vainly sought the shelter of the cup, pause for an instant and then return apologetically to our feet. So we continued our duel, scarcely needing to move our stance as the balls came back to us time and again, as if on elastic. Finally, one of them did drop, to our mutual delight, and we were able to move on to the next windswept tee.

I tactfully refrained from telling you before you played of the travail of Bobby Jones on his first encounter with the hole, in the 1921 Open. Legend had it that he put himself into Strath, where he played numerous shots before finally rocketing a ball out into the estuary. That, however, was untrue, as he confirmed on being granted the freedom of the city of St Andrews. It wasn't Strath at all, but Hill bunker. And he never had got out of that! I didn't want to undermine your confidence before your tee shot. Yes, I'm sure you're very grateful.

I'm quite convinced, as is always said, that confidence really is everything in golf. The psychological component must be greater than in any other game. I've no doubt that you find, like me, that you hit your best shots when you're not thinking about hazards ahead, or technique, or indeed anything at all. Watch that bush on the right! Oh dear, I'm in it. Or: must keep my head down! And up it comes. That's where your local pro gets it wrong. He insists on telling you what you must remember to do with your grip, or your stance, or your swing. What he should be doing, after earning his fee with good advice of this sort, is to suggest a technique for *forgetting* everything he's taught you, if only during those vital seconds while you make your stroke. An empty head is the first requirement for a successful shot. There's much to be said for the instruction imparted to an acquaintance, perhaps in despair, by a well-known pro he'd consulted: 'Oh, just go and hit the damned thing!'

WHINS

STROKE

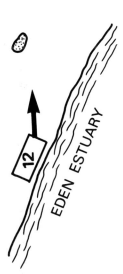

EDEN ESTUARY

HEATHERY (IN)

THIS LOOKS STRAIGHTFORWARD, DOESN'T IT? but I'm afraid it's here that the Old Course has reserved its most painful surprise for the uninitiated. You see that beautifully open fairway stretching all the way to the green? Well it isn't. Like a sinner on Sunday, it conceals its vices under a bland exterior; and the vices it's hiding are half a dozen ugly bunkers. The first, which you may remember from the seventh, is only just in front of the tee, so there's no need to worry about that. At driving length, however, and stretching across the heart of the fairway, is a big fellow called Stroke, with a little pot to its right. Should you, by dint of a burst of energy and a following wind, get over it, there are two more nasty pits beyond, with a further one cut into that hump in front of the green. In other words, an excellent drive on the pin is almost certainly doomed.

What's to be done, then? The pros tend to favour a long ball for the right end of the green, keeping left of that grassy bank with the bushes beyond; but that assumes a safe carry over the right-hand pot bunker. Mere mortals, on the other hand, can do worse than play for the left part of that bank, especially if the pin's well over on that side. But unless I'm in a slicing mood, I prefer, as usual, the left-hand route. This means going no further right than the heathery bank with its line of whins. Unless you're too far over towards the seventh tee, this leaves you with a sight of the long, narrow green; but at worst, as long as you don't get among the tussocks on the bank itself, you'll be left with a short iron over it. That will, though, need to be a well-judged shot to get up onto the raised surface of the green and hold there.

Now let's see if I can put my preaching into practice. — That's started off in the right direction, but it's fading a bit. Touch and go, I'd say, because Stroke does tend to collect them from that end. — Yes, go right by all means, if you feel happier; then you'll be able to come in to the right of that trap guarding the green. — And go right you certainly did! But don't worry; there's plenty of room over there, and the rough's not too bad. No, there's no out of bounds, not even if you finish on that green on the Eden where the children are putting. You simply take a free drop and pretend you'd come that way for the view.

*   *   *

I WAS ONCE PLAYING HERE very early in the morning in the days when it was a recognised thing to 'beat the ballot' in order to make sure of a round before the crowds arrived. That's a wonderful time to play, before the wind's got up, and with the dew still on the ground. Anyway, I could hardly believe my eyes when I saw a fellow staggering up that hill on our left (yes, the one on the seventh), carrying not only his bag, but his trolley too. He had enough breath left to return our 'Good mornings', and then plainly felt obliged to explain his eccentric behaviour. He was an American visitor who, like us, had begun his round before the arrival of the Starter, but without seeing the notice saying that trolleys are prohibited on the Old Course. It was on the fifth hole that Nemesis, in the shape of a ranger on his motor-bike, appeared and informed him in a few well-chosen words of the regulation. If he wanted to continue, said the ranger after accepting his green fee, he would have to carry his clubs. As it had been a long journey from California for the sake of just five holes, he elected to carry the clubs — in itself no great penance, except for the fact that they were in a rather outsize bag, and the bag was strapped to the trolley. He seemed remarkably cheerful in the circumstances.

Yes, golf has its ups and downs, which brings me to the

explanation I promised for the nickname 'the Admiral's bunker'. Where is it? You'll soon find out, if you leave the tee in that direction; and that would give more point to the story. The admiral in question was enjoying a carefree round in the sunshine at the time before trolleys were outlawed. As he set out from this tee, his eye was caught by a shapely young lady in pillar-box red wending her way up the seventh fairway. She may have reminded him of a letter he'd forgotten to post; but in any case, so mesmerised was he by the apparition that he failed to notice the chasm yawning before him. In he pitched, and down crashed his clubs and trolley on top of him. Not since the wreck of the Hesperus had there been such a spectacular foundering!

LECKIE

This, alas, is also the hole where Tom Watson began to ship water, metaphorically, in the 1984 Open. It was the last day, as you may remember; and for some reason he took my recommended left-hand route which is not, however, advised for players of his length of shot. He finished, of course, in the whins. His challenge, which had looked so strong after a splendid third round, finally collapsed with an imprudent iron played to the base of the wall on the seventeenth. For all of this, though he would deny it, I hold myself responsible.

He had taken a house a couple of doors from me for the period of the championship; and on that fateful morning I passed him as he was loading his clubs into the car. Exchanging a brief greeting and complimenting him on his achievement of the previous day, I pointed out, as co-creator and indeed namer of the street, that it had not yet provided the world with an Open Champion. 'Not yet?' said Tom with a smile. As I watched his last round mainly, it must be admitted, on television, I began to sense that I had placed too great a weight of responsibility on his shoulders: three putts on the fifth, a tentative eleventh as I recall, the whins on the twelfth. Sorry, Tom: there are burdens too great to ask any man to bear. It's with pleasure, though, that I remember the evening of that doom-laden day. Hearing voices from my garden, I looked across; and there was Tom on his doorstep, having a friendly chat with some of the local children, who had, it appeared, taken him a consolatory bunch of flowers.

Well, here we are on the green at last, you in three, isn't it? to my five (thanks to my getting out of Stroke straight into that little brute by the green, and under the face too). Last time I was here, at the bottom of the slope, I showed my own fragility under pressure. I'd just addressed my putt and voided my mind almost to the point of implosion, when my opponent casually remarked: 'It had better be a good one: you're being photographed.' He was joking of course — or was he? And does it matter anyway?

HOLE 12 : HEATHERY (in)

My voided mind became a beehive. The putt covered about four inches of the fifteen feet. I looked up in anguish; and there, sure enough, was a man with a camera pointed in my direction: a casual stroller, with his wife it seemed, wanting some shots of the local wildlife. Fortunately, it didn't look like a cine camera.

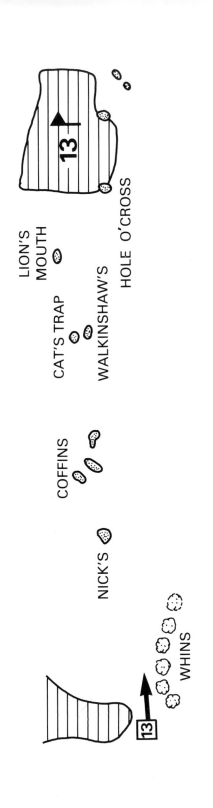

LION'S MOUTH

CAT'S TRAP

WALKINSHAW'S

HOLE O'CROSS

COFFINS

NICK'S

WHINS

13

HOLE 13

HOLE O'CROSS
(IN)

T HIS IS ANOTHER OF THE FEW HOLES WHERE 'IF
   you keep to the right you are wrong' doesn't apply.
The professionals, mind you, do play left, the reason being
that a long shot onto the sixth fairway gives you a clear sight
of the green at the end of a little valley. That line is more or
less on the sandy track you can see in the distance and from
here takes you just to the left of the group of bunkers called
the Coffins, which I mentioned earlier. Short of them is one
called Nick's. As it pre-dates Faldo and is quite a nasty one,
I suspect Old Nick of being its patron. That's the line, then,
if you want to show off or greet an acquaintance playing the
sixth.

For the prudent (and I've not quite summed you up
yet) I recommend the right-hand route. That's up the edge
of the fairway; and as the whins cut back quite a long way
from the line of those immediately ahead, there's a band of
reasonably innocuous rough before you get into them. From
there it's usually possible to hit a straight shot to the pin. I
said possible, not easy. This is the thirteenth, after all.

You have the honour back now, so it's you to fire. And
I promise not to tell your psychiatrist which line you take,
or to ask you which you've opted for before you drive. —
Aha, a well-balanced personality, it would appear. — And
after all that, I've followed you down the middle.

Now if you just come up on this hump, you'll see
what's left to be done. First you have to cross that plateau
and get over that shaggy bank beyond it; then you must
keep clear of the deep bunker (Hole o'Cross) that bites into

the green. At the same time you need to avoid if possible that grassy channel running up to the green and, even more urgently, the Lion's Mouth trap this side of it (I once saw a lady international take three or four to get out of there). Oh yes, it's a challenge: but would you want it otherwise? Langer, after all, hits balls out of trees.

Still, it's me to go. And what a mess: it hardly left the ground and will only just scramble across the plateau. — That's a better one of yours, although you've kicked off the mound towards the Lion's Mouth. I don't think you're quite in it, though. — Oh, no! See where I am! Let me introduce you to Walkinshaw's, whoever he was. Come to think of it, I read somewhere that he was a noted left-hander of the last century: and serve him right! It would take a left-hander or even a contortionist to get out of it from where I am.

*   *   *

SO WE BOTH GOT THERE IN THE END, even though I gave the folk putting out on the fifth a nasty fright when I thinned that wedge. And you won it with a seven? Oh dear! That prompts me to tell you of one of the few moments of glory I've had on this hole. I was playing on my own and had hit a good drive and an even better second, but unfortunately without looking to see if the green was clear. In fact it was not; but the threesome there, rather than taking offence, viewed me with admiration as I sneaked up to find my ball a foot or two from the hole. Deferentially they stood aside as I completed my birdie; and then, since one of them was a vague acquaintance, they asked me to join them for the rest of the round, if I would forgive their standard of golf. I graciously accepted their invitation, but couldn't fail to notice a diminution of their respect as the acquaintance ripened — and I failed to finish another hole in less than six.

Despite this being the thirteenth, I associate it with a string of only minor disasters, nothing really memorable.

One of my sons, though, once came close to causing a government crisis here. I thought it tactful not to mention when we were on the tee that our position there was dangerously exposed to sliced drives from the Eden course. The hole in question (it was the fifth at that time, before the course was remodelled) is a longish dog-leg to the green you came near to visiting on the twelfth. Having hit a rather poor drive, my son was determined to cut the dog-leg with his second, despite my warning that there was a group of people on the tee here. His second shot was very creditable and luckily had fair elevation, because it passed more or less over the group which, on closer inspection, I saw contained the bulky figure of the then Home Secretary.

The situation was reversed, with me as the fortunate survivor, when on another occasion I had tried the left-hand route here. As I was about to play my second, a ball from the sixth tee whistled over my head and went bounding down the fairway. Though startled, I had to admire the length achieved by the unseen driver. Scarcely had I recovered my poise, when this gladiator of the links appeared: a slight and lissom blonde, covered in blushes and apologetic confusion. Then I remembered that a ladies' championship was to be played the following day. Yes, it's timing, not brute force that does the trick.

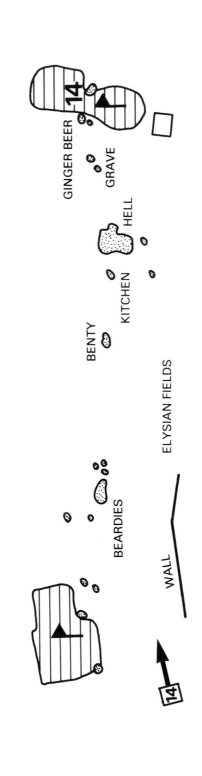

GINGER BEER

GRAVE

HELL

KITCHEN

BENTY

ELYSIAN FIELDS

BEARDIES

WALL

14

HOLE 14

LONG HOLE

I F YOU'VE RECOVERED YOUR COMPOSURE, WE'LL tackle the so-called Long Hole, which is actually not much longer than the fifth, though rather more hazardous. Like so many of the holes on this course, it calls for a strategic, not a bull-at-a-gate approach. That's why opinions on the merits of the Old are so sharply divided. The blood-and-thunder players tend to hate it, because it's apt to trump what they consider their best tricks; but the crafty finaglers, stealthy planners, avoiders of the spectacular but adepts at the sneaky 'St Andrews shots' (especially the low chip and run) are loud in their praise. Most of us, I need hardly say, just play it for fun.

What's my own strategy? It's largely determined by the drive, so let's concentrate on that. Yes, concentrate; head down, smooth swing and all that. The first target is the fairway, which doesn't need a long carry from here, so there's no need to try and knock the cover off the ball. It's a different matter from the tiger tee: that's it in the distance behind you, the small platform in front of that stone bench dedicated to Alex Ayton. (He was the youngest member of the well-known Ayton family and made a name for himself in the States.) Perched up there, you gaze round 'with a wild surmise' like stout Cortez and his men from their peak in Darien; and you wonder where on earth the fairway can be. It lies, in fact, between the wall bounding the Eden and a menacing group of bunkers called the Beardies, the largest of which is as profound as the despair of the unlucky golfer who lands in it. A quick hook might get you into that heathery basin on the left, which you avoided when finishing off on the fifth. Bury yourself in there, and you have real problems. So line up on the right-hand church spire, head down, and shoot!

Fine! You're a bit left of the spire, but not far enough over to be drawn into the Beardies, I think. In fact you're nicely set up for your next shot. — Ah, I've cut mine badly: that will finish near the wall. So as I am not likely to see much more of you before the green, I'd better tell you how to get there before we go our several ways.

Play your next one over the bank and down onto the fifth fairway. From there, depending on your length, you should have a reasonble chance of reaching the green. Don't slice it, though, because as this is a friendly game I'd hate to see you in Hell. You don't know about Hell (as a religious lady once asked me on a street corner)? Yes, it's a bunker all right; and if you ever went to Sunday School, you can imagine what a huge, cavernous place it is — as big as a green on a normal course. My advice is to follow Dante's example: take a look and pass on. Mind you, unless you're up against the face or, worst of all, in the little nose to the left, you're not irrevocably lost: a good shot from a decent lie could spell your salvation, and even put you on the green. Too far left, though, could land you in one of a pair of bunkers called Grave — the only way known to mortals of proceeding from Hell to the Grave and not vice versa. (It was the switching of the direction of the course that created this anomaly, which shows the antiquity of many of the names.) To complete the infernal topography, I should mention Hell's Kitchen, which lies in front of the dreaded pit. Less sinister, perhaps, though further left, is Ginger Beer bunker, cutting into the green and presumably in the vicinity of where the beverage I mentioned on the fourth used to be dispensed. You'll see when you get there that there's quite a steep bank at the front of the green and an awkward hump at its right end, after which it slopes away to the back. If you're short, this is a good place to practise your chip and runs.

As I'm so far right, I'll have to try a different route.

HOLE 14 : LONG HOLE

You won't be surprised to learn that the flat open fairway ahead is known as the Elysian Fields. It's best not to stray beyond them, because they end with a steep, rough bank — more a slippery slope than a primrose path down to Hell; and there are even a couple of traps over there. If, from where I am, you must flaunt your prowess with a fairway wood and have virtue enough to keep to the straight and narrow, then you might go for the extreme right-hand end of the bank; but it's a perilous passage, and the safety of your soul isn't guaranteed. However, that's my problem today, not yours. So you go your way and I'll go mine; and let's hope we meet again in the blessed thereafter.

*   *   *

SO HERE WE ARE AT LAST! In how many? — That's not bad. I decided to risk it down the right; and although I missed the whins, my ball found a cosy nest in the rough, and you saw the nasty kick I got off that hump. Anyway, what's wrong with an eight? No worse than Jack Nicklaus. Yes, I saw him tot up an eight here once. It was in one of those matches for television. He hit a long, raking drive which landed out of bounds just the wrong side of the wall. With his next ball, he over-compensated and finished in that little pot bunker at the end of the Beardies, from which he took two to get out. Then onto the green with an iron, and two putts for an eight. It happens to the best of us, even if, unlike that famous bishop, we don't stray into Hell on the way.

What famous bishop? You don't know the favourite St Andrews story? Well, that worthy man of the purple cloth, who counted golf among his chief religious activities, found himself in the infernal sands. Whereupon his caddie, one of the old breed and a man of few words, gave his considered advice: 'Tak' yer niblick, my lord!' — 'No, my mashie, I think,' said the bishop, putting his faith in a less down-to-earth guide; 'I think I can reach the green from here.' — 'Yer niblick', growled the caddie, his hand on the

implement. — 'No, my mashie, if you please.' Unused to any flouting of his judgment, the caddie grudgingly handed him his chosen club. The bishop swung it like a censer, and the ball flew miraculously out of Hell and onto the green. The scowling caddie cocked his eye at the triumphant prelate: 'If I was you, my lord,' he declared, 'I'd be buried wi' yon club!'

How good are you on the rules? Try this one, then. I once hit a ball from the Elysian Fields into the Beardies. What? — Yes, I was going backwards in a sense: I should explain that during some past winters the course has been played in reverse, for the sake of its health. You may think it odd, but that was the traditional way of tackling it: there is, for instance, an early nineteenth-century plan of 'Pilmoor Links' showing ten holes played that way and finishing near the present turn, and with the sea where the present New and Jubilee courses now lie. But back to that point of the rules. My partner had played first; then I followed on the same line. When we arrived at the Beardies, we found both balls in the sand. What's more, his was in the bottom of a deep pit, apparently made by a passing elephant's hoof, whilst mine was sitting on its back, fractionally further from the hole. My shot; but I would have to hit his ball. And if he moved it, mine would have dropped from a virtually to a totally impossible lie. I won't go on; but you see the difficulty. There must be an answer, if it's only that elephants should be kept off the golf course.

Here's another one to try you out; and this time there's a genuine solution. It happened not here but in Crail, although the victim told me about it after a round here. The previous day he had been playing in a friendly four-ball, with no strokes given, and no quarter either, it seemed. For he had achieved the golfer's dream: a hole in one! Yet his opponents claimed the hole. Why? – Oh look, we're holding these chaps up. See if you can work out the answer before the next green.

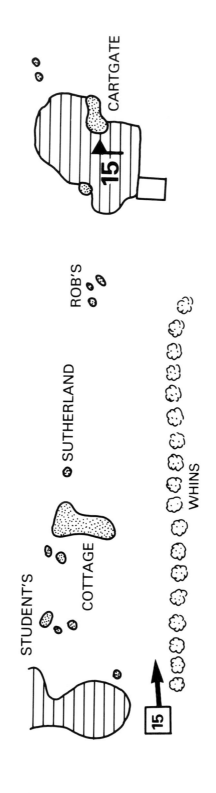

HOLE 15

CARTGATE (IN)

THE LINE HERE IS FOR THE GAP BETWEEN THE two banks you see ahead. There's just one snag: unless you hit a good one, you may find yourself in the Cottage — no, not the one back there: that's the toilets nowadays; and even my shanking friend could hardly get one to go 170° off line! What I'm referring to is a great shallow Saharan depression stretching across the fairway from the end of the right-hand hill. It presents no problems unless you're under the lip (the sand is pretty hard), but it would be a bit humbling to end up there in today's conditions, when a reasonable drive should carry it. Even more galling would be to fly it safely, only to see your ball go into Sutherland's, the little pot lurking beyond. So if you want to be safe, hit one only just off the end of that hill. Be warned, though: a slice would take you round these first whins to a bay of tussocky rough, with another bank of bushes to the right of that.

Your second, from wherever you land, is likely to be more or less over a group of small traps known as Rob's. However, after a reasonable drive the chief problem is not so much reaching the green, but getting the right distance to the pin. Did you notice from the third green how far back it was? I think it was fairly near the front, where there are some tricky borrows. In general the green slopes from the bank of the bunker down to the right; so the best line in is usually just to the left of the flag. Away you go, then. And you're two up.

*   *   *

A CHAT ROUND THE OLD COURSE

THE FIRST TIME I EVER USED a Golden Ram ball was from the medal tee here. I hit one of my typical low ones, and there was a report like a firecracker as the ball impacted on the tee-box ahead. We all ducked in a reflex of self-preservaton; but astonishingly none of us saw what happened to the ball. Nor did we find it, although we searched in ever-widening circles round the tee. — Caught in a thicket, we supposed.

If so, it was in those bushes to our right; and that was where I made my most pathetically moving discovery on any golf course. From the depths of the whins (no, please don't ask what I was doing there — where's your tact?) I retrieved what appeared to be a brand-new putter: brand-new, but sadly mutilated. The toe had been sawn completely off! One needs little imagination to guess what had happened. — 'Happy birthday, Dad! I knew you wanted a putter. This should cure your trouble.' — 'Did it do the trick, Dad? Well, I'm sure you'll get the feel of it if you persevere.' — 'Where's that putter I gave you, Dad? Oh, never mind: I expect someone will hand it in.' It's just as well that the donor wasn't present to witness the scene as Father, quitting the fourteenth green apoplectic with rage after his four putts from ten feet, hurled the offending love-gift to perdition. To have it returned would inevitably have spelt the end of his family life, or his golfing career, or his sanity, or more probably of all three.

Yes, those crows remained remarkably unruffled when you almost hit them. But they always do. And have you noticed the great expressive range of their vocabulary? That pair gave you a most blasphemous croak; but when they're chatting to each other, their vocabulary changes from forthright caws to quiet grumblings and everything in between. The ornithologically minded will tell you they're not crows at all, but rooks. In 'guid Scots', though, they're all 'craws' or 'damn' craws'. However, I'll let you into a secret; for it's my belief that they're all reincarnations of those old St Andrews caddies. Just listen to their talk. And watch the way they hop along, cursing as they go — not to mention their dress. I once had virtual proof of my theory. I was standing behind the eighteenth green watching a party finishing their round. One of the balls lay in a hollow just short of the green, hidden from its owner, as was the 'craw' that sidled up to it. The bird gave it a sharp peck, and it rolled a few inches forward. Then another peck, and another, trundling it along until it was on the putting surface. With its mission accomplished, the crow cawed with satisfaction and flapped away. Why had it done that? The only rational explanation, surely, is that it was reverting to its behaviour in that previous existence as a caddie who, with the size of his tip very much in mind, would use fair means or foul to help his own man.

Oh yes: how had my friend had an 'ace' and still lost the hole? You've not guessed? Well, he was playing a blind par three. All four of the party had hit their tee shots, one of which might have found the rough near the green, whilst he thought his own was a bit short and to the right. While his partner went to hunt in the rough, there being only three balls visible, he played the one he assumed to be his. You can imagine his jubilation when it transpired that his tee shot had been in the hole all the time! And then his woe when it was pointed out that the hole was not concluded until the balls involved had been properly identified; and therefore, having played the wrong one, he had lost the hole the moment he did so.

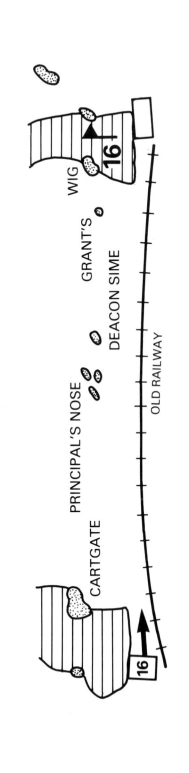

WIG

GRANT'S

DEACON SIME

PRINCIPAL'S NOSE

OLD RAILWAY

CARTGATE

16

16

CORNER OF THE DYKE

YOU'RE STILL TWO UP, THEN; AND IT'S HIGH TIME I made my move. This isn't the best hole for it, as there's very little trouble I can neglect to warn you about. There, at driving length, is the Principal's Nose, which I pointed out on the third. What you can't see from here are the two 'nostrils' immediately behind it, waiting for the bold intended carry or the shot that seems to tweak the Nose and get away with it. And beyond it, immediately to its right, is Deacon Sime, ready to receive even the mildly deviant into his den for a painful interview. Over the fence on what used to be the second hole of the Eden (alas for its passing!) is, of course, out of bounds.

So where do you aim? Prudence counsels a safe route well to the left, which is the way most professionals play it nowadays. The only reason for hesitation is that the line for the second shot then runs closer to two bunkers: Grant's, just short of the green, and the larger Wig, which eats into it. If you play to avoid them and put a bit of a cut on the ball, you could well finish uncomfortably close to the fence. The green, by the way, is fairly flat once you're on the top level. There is a slope, though, down from the second hole; and, more to the point, the low banks on the other three sides can encourage the running ball into adjacent gullies.

For the bold and foolhardy the tight drive between Nose and fence is a tempting prospect, to which I often succumb. In that case, I tee my ball low so that it remains unaware of the freedom it could enjoy in the great wide yonder. My memory suggests that the old masters (and Kel

Nagle in particular comes to mind) used to take that line more often. But they had the skill to launch a long ball over the Eden and draw it back across the fence to finish in the perfect spot. Ah, the things we could all do in our dreams!

*   *   *

DO YOU EVER HAVE NIGHTMARES about the game? One of my partners once told me of a very bizarre one, which had caused him to wake in sheer panic. He was faced with a shot to a broad green tilting slightly towards him. Having selected his wedge and addressed the ball, he looked up to find the green now spread with white damask and laid out as if for a banquet, with magnificent silverware and wine glasses, flowers in porcelain vases and, where the hole should have been, a priceless crystal decanter. It's a situation rarely encountered in real life, thank goodness.

As I'm sure you know, that track on the other side of the fence used to be the railway line for those many years (how far away they seem!) when St Andrews enjoyed such a link with the outside world. The first two and last two holes of the Eden course lay to the south of it, the remainder to the north; and the two parts were joined by a steep footbridge eighty yards or so behind this sixteenth tee. Its removal was the only advantage I can think of for the golfer; for at the end of a hard round it proved quite a commando-style obstacle for the flagging devotee encumbered by a ponderous trolley. Only such as the American I mentioned on the twelfth could have made light of it.

The presence of the railway certainly added a spice of excitement both for those playing this hole and for the travellers rash enough to lean out of their carriage windows as they rumbled by. Courtesy as well as simple humanity would normally cause the golfer to hold his fire in such situations; but the occasional light engine, free of its string of coaches, was fair game. With a well-timed shank into the tender, you could, invoking the rub of the green, claim to have hit a shot that either circled the coast of Fife or else landed up behind you at Leuchars junction.

As well as the passing of the railway, I much regret the removal of a cryptic notice at a crossing gate for vehicles just by the seventeenth tee. Seemingly intended for those with an exceptionally long reach, it read: 'STOP, LOOK, LISTEN! OPEN FAR GATE BEFORE CROSSING.'

Other than adventures involving the railway and its traffic, the most impressive trick shot that I've seen played on the sixteenth was the work of that gentleman I earlier referred to as D.D. It was a good, firm drive straight for the Principal's Nose, which it struck, appropriately enough, well up on the face. The ball leapt high into the air, dropped vertically, and after a single bounce came to rest precariously on the very bridge of the Nose. Just look when you pass it, and you'll realise how little room there is for the ball, let alone for the one who had to play it from its perch.

Drive away, then; but don't try to emulate that feat! — No, you haven't; I'm afraid it's just curled in. You may find you have to play out towards the fence. If so, be careful not to go through it. It wasn't long ago that I saw a championship round wrecked like that.

Well, you did the best you could from there. But that's one back to me: my charge has begun.

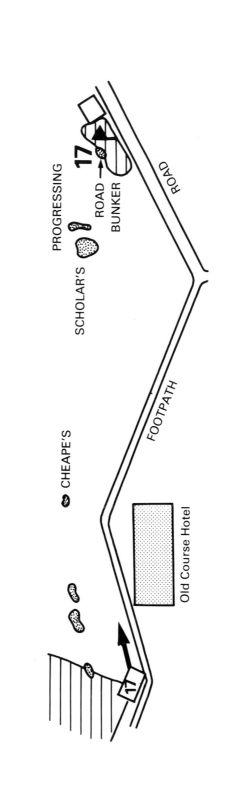

PROGRESSING

SCHOLAR'S

CHEAPE'S

17

ROAD →
BUNKER

ROAD

FOOTPATH

Old Course Hotel

17

HOLE 17

ROAD HOLE

T HIS IS THE ONE YOU'VE BEEN WAITING FOR! WAS that why you let me take that hole: to avoid having the honour here? It's variously described as the best, or the most difficult, par four in golf. You can make up your own mind, which will probably depend on the number of shots you take. How are you feeling? Let's take it bit by bit, then.

The drive, as you see, is an adventure in its own right. Had you been brimming with confidence and sure of a long hit, I'd have advised you to go over that wooden shed, cutting off twenty feet or so of the dog-leg (the wall angles back round the corner). In the old days the line was a tall chimney in the distance; but that was before they built the hotel. So don't try to bite off too much or, especially with a fade, you're likely to find yourself in the duck pond. — Oh, you didn't know about that? Sorry for mentioning it! Although I call it a duck pond, word seems to have got around in feathered circles that it's a risky place to linger, what with golf balls descending from the sky and the appraising glances of diners from the hotel windows. Anyway, I've seen no ducks there for some time.

What was there before the hotel? I'll tell you that later. If your nerve fails you, or you're using the last ball in your bag, I'd suggest you go left of the shed. But where to? That's the problem. If you can thread the ball through by the end of the path, that's fine. Be ready, though, to stop in mid-swing if you see any of those casual promenaders appear round the corner. They come in more varieties than Messrs Heinz ever dreamed of: men with walking-sticks and binoculars, Japanese gentlemen with cameras, hikers with rucksacks, business executives wrapped in conversation and dark raincoats, elderly ladies with dogs on leads, young ladies with nothing much on at all, the inevitable pram-pusher, children on bikes, courting couples with eyes only for each other, groups of bird-watchers — in fact anything nowadays but train-spotters.

Should you not relish the prospect of giving evidence at an inquest, you could always aim further left: much further, because Cheape's bunker lies at about eleven o'clock to the end of the wall; and although it's fairly shallow, it will cost you a lot of distance. Get past that, and you're on the second fairway, but with a very long way still to go. Right, I'll try and keep my head down for this drive more than any other!

Well, despite all my dire warnings, we're both in reasonable shape; but there's no hope of reaching the green from here. What we should aim to do is put our seconds as near to the right-hand edge of the fairway as possible, but without going through into the rough, which is usually long and clinging just there. That to the left isn't much better: full of hummocks and spots where the ball can bed down for the night. It's quite possible to lose a ball on either side; but to the left is the additional hazard of a couple of bunkers: Scholar's full of its own importance and very firm sand as a rule, and Progressing (it sounds like a scholar's report, doesn't it?).

Yes, we're progressing too. This line, as you see, gives us a reasonable shot along the length of the green. It's best to play a little right of the pin, as there's a slight slope down from the road side. Yes: that could be good if it holds. Oh, bad luck: it was running just too strongly. But better on the road than in the Road Bunker, the notorious 'sands of Nakajima'. You probably saw that on television. My heart bled for the unfortunate fellow, especially as I'd done the very same thing not long before: putted up from the side of the green, misread the slope, found myself swept into the sand, and yo-yoed up and down half-a-dozen times before I got out onto *terra firma*. — Oh yes, you're allowed to ground your club on the road. At least you're not up against the wall like poor Tom Watson, or in the donkey paddock over it. A firm putt sometimes does the trick from where you are. You never know: this may be your lucky day. — Not bad at all! — But my five just scrapes it.

*　　*　　*

YOU ASKED EARLIER what was there before the arrival of the hotel (which, by the way, was built by British Rail to virtually coincide with the closure of the line). The answer is a railway depot, with sidings and a group of black sheds, whose removal changed the whole character of the drive on this hole. To keep a shadow of the time-honoured sheds, a metal framework was erected in the original shape, and from it was draped green netting. It incorporated a canopy in which misguided balls were apt to collect. A year or two ago the netting was replaced by the present structure.

Long before all this development, I was told a story about a drive from this tee which I found hard to credit. The perpetrator, so it was said, was a local golfer whom we'll call J.B.G. To the right of the tee were the first and last fairways of the Eden course, bounded on the far side by a stone wall, beyond which ran the then main road to Cupar. On the other side of that road and over another wall were playing fields. Well, J.B.G., so I was assured, had hit his drive with such misplaced adroitness that his ball had finished in those playing fields, without human or mechanical intervention. Perhaps you noticed the fields, which are still where they were then. Now I've heard many golfing stories in my time. But there are limits to even my credulity.

One day three of us came across a singleton waiting for a game, and we invited him to join us. He introduced himself as 'J.B.G.' As we walked down the first fairway, I broached the subject: 'Someone once told me a story about you: pure nonsense, of course.' — 'About my drive from the seventeenth?' — 'Yes.' — 'Absolutely true,' he said, and went on to tell me how it happened. He had hit a considerable slice, which had taken the ball to the platform by the goods depot (that is, to the right of the present hotel). From there it had bounded at almost ninety degrees onto the tarmac in front of the Eden starter's box, whence a series of kangaroo hops had taken it across the wall to the road and finally into the playing fields. Golfers, like fishermen, are not to be disbelieved.

Indeed, this is one of those holes where even the most discreet of players is liable to indulge in moments of wild abandon. You can tell the sort who would leave their cars at home when going to a party, because they are the ones who furtively select the oldest ball in the bag for their drive: a sure sign that they intend to let their hair down for once. Many are the balls over the years that have bid their final farewells with a mocking whistle as they flew from the seventeenth tee. The old black sheds were always reluctant to surrender their prey. Then, when the hotel came, the original stone balconies waited for titbits like animals at feeding time and never, to my knowledge, disgorged a thing. From the canopy over the original front door a ball would gain new impetus, as when a space shot fires its second stage, and seek refuge or refreshment by the Jigger Inn. I have watched others hit the lofty chimney at the end of the building, never to be seen again. And now, of course, the pond collects offerings like a wishing well (I have heard surely apocryphal stories of waiters retiring on the proceeds). Sometimes, though, you might have actually recovered your ball, if in a most unexpected place, as when my son retrieved his from under a helicopter (parked beyond the netting where the sheds now are). And one used to see grown men gazing up like small boys at a neighbour's apple tree, then hurling their clubs to try to dislodge the balls collected by the net rather further along.

In short, if ever one feels a miracle coming on, this is the hole to perform it. Even so, one had to take with a pinch of salt, just after that astronaut had rehearsed the basic moves of the game on earth's satellite, the ball that appeared, set in a newly pointed piece of the wall by the seventeenth green, with the rough inscription: 'Shepard's shot from the moon'. Several times the ball disappeared, and I replaced it with another, but only for that to vanish in its turn. However, when I last visited the spot, a few yards short of the green, I was delighted to see once again a ball embedded in the mortar, although the inscription has almost weathered away. It was good to find that some noble conservationist, after so many battles fought and lost in this home of golf, is determined to preserve at least that small remnant of the time-honoured scenario. — Look, there it is! The ball seems suspiciously new, I grant, after such a journey. Maybe NASA should be approached with a view to adopting and maintaining that historic piece of masonry.

To return to more terrestrial matters, perhaps you may remember my account of the denting of D.D.'s four iron on the third and that I promised you the sequel on the seventeenth. Well, D.D. was left with a crucial shot to this green; and for it he selected his trusty four iron. With his usual panache and vigour, he swung the club-head through the ball, which departed with less than its usual velocity when the shaft snapped clean through at the point of the dent. His insurance company, I gather, proved very sympathetic.

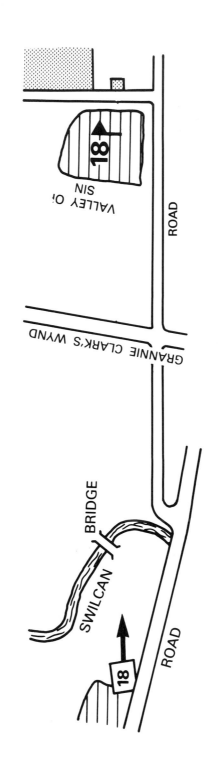

TOM MORRIS HOLE

HERE WE ARE, THEN: NO MORE BUNKERS OR bushes; and with the burn at our feet, these acres of fairway beckoning, and the nineteenth hole only just over the horizon, surely all the day's disasters (such as they were) are behind us. What's more, the sun's still shining, and we're all square.

For once, the placing of the tee doesn't make much difference. Today we're to the left, which adds a yard or two, but that's of no significance: wherever you play from, the favourite line is for the monument or the R. and A. clock; but as long as you trundle the ball well down the fairway, it doesn't much matter where you finish. With this breeze behind us and the ground quite firm, the road's just about in range. If you go for it, for the sake of your macho image and the spectators hanging around outside the Woollen Mill, don't excite yourself into a slice. The cars beyond the railings are strictly out of bounds, though it's not so very many years ago that that part of the road was unfenced and consequently within the playing area. That, of course, still applies to the road running across from Grannie Clark's Wynd (no, I know nothing more about that worthy grandam); and you can claim no relief from the tarmac, should you finish there.

I'll not wait for that family party on their way back from the beach: my shots can't be lethal at that range. — Oh, why did I have to spot them? I never hook like that on this hole! But I'm still inside the railings, so that will do. In fact it's a stroke of luck, as I wanted to arrange a tie with that chap just leaving the first tee. — What an excellent shot of yours! I don't think it quite reached the road, but it did make them turn round in admiration.

Before our ways divide, I'd better say something about the green: you won't want me to be giving you hints under the eyes of that admiring mini-gallery. They're all your supporters, I suppose? Well, you'll have noticed from the first tee the deep hollow in front of the green; it's the famous Valley of Sin, for obvious reasons. You must try to get onto the top level, either directly with a pitch or with that local brand of run-up. Beware, though, of going up the bank at the back. The ball almost always sticks there; and it's by no means easy to hack it down to the vicinity of the hole. I remember watching Nicklaus play that shot (not a hack in his case) — but he'd got there with his drive! Even when you're nicely on the green, you'll find the slopes quite hard to judge: I think it must be something to do with the line of the banks and fences on this best-known of all golfing stagesets. Or perhaps it's because of the feeling that every critical spectator knows much better than you which way the ball's going to borrow.

*   *   *

THE MOST HANDSOME DRIVE I've ever seen from this tee was by Sevvy Ballesteros; and yet he never holed out. Yes, you've guessed: it was in a practice round, in company with his brother — 'Go on, Sevvy, drive the green!' He put all his power and rhythm into the shot. The ball started out over the road; and as we all gasped, it drew back across the fence, pitched short and ran up by the pin (the hole was cut to the right) to finish about six feet past. When Sevvy reached the green, he putted and missed, then did a fair impersonation of a man with the yips before picking up with a shrug and a smile.

If only we could all control our drives like that! I mentioned some of the wild ones I'd seen from the seventeenth tee, generated, I suspect, as much by a sense of panic as by a surge of 'fine careless rapture'. On this last hole, dazzled by the sight of the light at the end of the tunnel and determined to achieve at least one memorable stroke in the round, the golfer is inclined to see himself in the role of Ballesteros on course for the Open. He may not go as far as one of my companions, who once put such momentum into his shot that he swung himself off his feet and headed the ball off the tee. Nevertheless, he is liable to retain the same degree of control as a car on a skidpan and despatch the ball to unthought-of places. To see one leave the course en route for the beach is not unknown; and I have witnessed a hook so fearsome into an easterly gale that it crossed the burn twice to finish out of bounds near the Himalayas. I wouldn't claim any particular distinction for drives of my own that have dived for cover under the ancient stone bridge or for one which I hit on the head so that it hopped the Swilcan three times at its meander before finding a safe haven on the fairway. More spectacular was my son's 'resurrection shot' which sent the ball into the burn to strike the further bank with a crack and a splash at the point where it met the water. A further crack announced that it had rebounded to the nearer bank, whereupon it arose like Lazarus to nestle gratefully on the grass beyond.

I was, I must admit, more proud of my pushed slog which rifled into that large window in the end house and catapulted back to a perfectly playable lie a yard or two in front of the medal tee to the right. That is the more common direction for these erratic shots to take, which is why I never park my car on the road beyond the railings. I learned that lesson early, when I saw one headlamp lying in fragments on the road; but to the eternal credit of the culprit, he had left his scorecard complete with name and address stuffed into the hole his ball had made. On a later occasion I was standing on the road when there was an explosion too close for comfort. A ball had just shattered a windscreen, then rebounded onto the fairway. Without a twitch of the lips or a sideways glance, its owner (of the ball, that is, not the car) strolled up, played his second casually to the green, and no doubt finished with a par as well as the car to his credit, if that's the word. Yes, balls fly fast and free along that stretch of the road. The other day I saw one lodged in the guttering of that white house, and at a point totally invisible from the tee. When I recently complimented an official of the New Club next door on his good fortune in leaving his car there with never an obvious dent, he replied: 'It's funny you should say that, because only yesterday someone asked me if I'd prised that ball out of my radiator yet.'

Some drives fly wider still. I have myself seen one pitch on the road to the right of the houses and, like J.B.G.'s from the seventeenth, traverse the main thoroughfare to disappear into a front garden beyond. Before those white railings went up, the local out of bounds rules were not very clearly defined. I've always envied the composure of my late friend George (the only person I've ever beaten 10 and 8, though I have to add that a couple of days later, when I played him in a match, he gave me two strokes and won 2 and 1). You'll gather that his golf lacked consistency; and that was especially true of his driving. Anyway, he once sliced his tee shot onto the main road. Quite unabashed, he took his putter and propelled the ball from there down Grannie Clark's Wynd and thence to the green to complete the hole.

Strange things can happen to second shots, too. The friend who balanced his ball, you remember, on the bridge of the Principal's Nose, once achieved the virtually impossible here as well. After a short drive, he scooped his next shot high into the air, so that the ball dropped more or less perpendicularly onto the road, whence it took vertical flight and continued to bounce up and down, all forward momentum lost, until it finally came to rest, still on the road. At least no offence was caused that time. But when he once carved one over the wall into Rusack's Hotel car park, he there encountered a woman furiously brandishing the projectile and exclaiming 'Would you mind keeping your balls on your lawn!'

The most amusing incident I've seen on this hole, and in which I was powerless to intervene, I witnessed from behind the reinforced window of the New Club. I happened to be looking out as two fairly rough-hewn golfers played their final drives. One of the shots was mediocre; but the other player clearly thought he had surpassed himself, as the triumphant waving of a clenched fist testified. In fact, though he couldn't see it from the tee, his ball had finished on the road. Seemingly in no hurry, the amiable twosome indulged in some back-chat and back-slapping before eventually shouldering their clubs and leaving the teeing ground. What they hadn't noticed were two women strolling across from the direction of the West Sands. They came to the ball on the road; and one of them, after picking it up and examining it with the interest of someone quite unfamiliar with the sport, replaced it on the tarmac and walked on. But then, as if struck by a pang of conscience, she went back and picked it up again, looking round to see who might have mislaid it. The only golfers she could spot were a couple with their backs turned as they putted out on the green. A kindly soul, thinking only of doing them a good turn, she threw the ball as best she could towards them, then rejoined her friend and proceeded innocently off the course. It was only then that our two hearties left the tee. The first played his next shot, while his companion went to look for his own ball. This way and that he went, but could find no trace of it. Where could it be? His friend walked forward and then began to wave frantically: he had discovered it on the green, in the Valley of Sin. Oh, what a scene of exulation I watched then. Not one fist was waved, but two; backs must have smarted under all the slaps. No Open winner can ever have looked so jubilant — to have driven the last green, and at St Andrews! Had I not been shut in behind that sealed window, what would I have done? Told him what I had seen and soured the supreme moment of his golfing career? Never! He's doubtless still dining out on that single shot, which outshines by far all others he has ever played or, unless he has retired on the strength of it, ever will.

But here we are on the green ourselves. Yes, I did manage to fix my match up: adjacent fairways have their uses as well as their perils. That really was a splendid shot of yours. Playing to the gallery, eh? I must say, I was quite pleased with my own; but you're well inside me. — Ah, one of my better putts. — Hey! You've sunk it! That's more than poor Doug Sanders did from just about the same spot. A very fair result, then: a squared match. — But no, of course that was a birdie of yours! I thought the applause from the gallery was a bit overdone. What a way to finish!

The least I can do after that is to take you to the nineteenth to toast your victory. You will come to the club for a pint or a tot (or both), won't you? Then you can tell me all about your own home club. I might drop in for the return match some time, who knows? I've always fancied a game in Australia.

I make your score 91, by the way; but we'd better get off the green to check it. Let's swagger off with those cheers still ringing in our ears. I do hope I didn't bore you with all the chat: at least it doesn't seem to have put you off your game. And if you've enjoyed it half as much as I have, then you're a very happy man!

NOTES

NOTES

NOTES

NOTES